VIOLA

A look at Non-physical Violence in Relationships

What is Relationship Violence?
What Causes it?
How do we Prevent it?

Spartacus R.

offers some liberating answers
for both men and women

SUKISA PUBLICATIONS
LONDON
1995

ISBN 1-870819-02-0

First published in England 1995
by Sukisa Publications Ltd.
25 Hayter Road,
Brixton,
London SW2 5AR
Tel: 0171 737 8280
Fax: 0171 924 0934

Design, layout, artwork and cover art by SukisArt

Back Cover Photograph by Xana

British Library Cataloguing-in-Publication Data
R., Spartacus
Violation: a look at non-physical Violence in Relationships: what is Relationship Violence? what causes it? how do we prevent it?
Spartacus R offers some liberating answers for both men and women.
1. Violence, Domestic Violence, Spousal Abuse, Women, Men, Relationships, Information and Communication,
Indexed

Printed in England by Biddles Ltd, Guildford.

This book is dedicated to the living memory of:

Sylvia Mary Bedeau
and
Theophilus Bedeau
and
Shango Shangane Bedeau

Other published works by Spartacus R. include:

the first three Osibisa albums, 'Osibisa' in 1971, 'Woyaya' in 1972, and 'Heads' - 1973 on MCA records;

four solo albums, 'Watching You Grow' in 1976, 'Africa I See' - 1982 (on cassette only) 'Third World War' - 1983 and 'Freedom First' - 1984 and singles not released on any albums including the 12" 45s 'Mother Sucker'/'Stop Your Crying' - 1979, 'Jamahiriya: (Africa Will Be Free)' /'Woza Malcolm: (Have They All Become Americans?)' 1986 and '2-4-1'/'Soca Carnival' -1988 all on the Zara Music Records label and published by Ekko Myah Music;

production credits for 'Thunder Into Our Hearts' by Jabula and 'Dis Policeman' by Benjamin Zephania both on Virgin Records;

literary works, 'Love and Life: a collection of songs, poems and thoughts' - 1988 and 'The Human Value' - 1987 both published by Sukisa Publications and periodical essays reviewing and previewing the decades of the 80s and 90s entitled: "1980" and "Towards 2000" respectlively;

journalistic works published in various African magazines including:

editing and writing articles for **Global Africa Pocket News** Magazine which started publication in January 1994.

Acknowledgements

Thanks and praises to the Ancestors.

I am eternally grateful to all those who have helped and guided me throughout my life, in particular, my **parents** to whose memory this book is dedicated, and all who have helped in the completion of this project. Especially, I would like to thank:

all my **children** for being; **Xana** for being there and helping to save my life; **Clement** for caring; **Chris** for commenting so honestly on the dissertation and book draft; **Bob**, you'll never know how much; **Leroy** for trying; **Bernard** for constructive criticism of the dissertation.

My deepest gratitude to the following friends, colleagues and associates, without whose devastating, challenging and constructive criticism of the first draft, this book would not be of the standard it is (don't blame them for it though): Brother **Femi Biko**, Brother **Kubara**, Brother **Ntum Lester Lewis**, Brother **Dr. Osakwe Osifo**, Sister **Patricia Agana**.

Apologies to those of you whose names I did not mention. It is not because your contribution was not valued, it is merely that I have failed to show my appreciation in that manner but hopefully, will be able to do so in some other satisfying way.

A special 'thank you' to the unnameable people who gave up their valuable time to fill up the questionnaires and those who gave more of themselves to answer more unanswerably painful questions face to face. Thanks to the professionalism and generosity of **Luke Daniels, Jillian Walton** and "**Mary**".

Also, I would like to thank everyone who wanted to help but for whatever reasons, found it impossible to do so.

Love and Life,
Spartacus R.

Preface

This book is based on research undertaken for an undergraduate dissertation project at the University of North London, England in 1992, entitled:

"Relationship Violence:

Information Needs of Couples in Relationships with Physical and/or Non-Physical Violence: the Quality and Quantity of Information they Receive on the Nature, Causes and Prevention of Violence in Relationships, Including 'Non-Violent' Relationships"

It is not, by any means, the definitive statement on non-physical violence, but at the time the research was undertaken, there was not and still there is not, as far as we know, any other research undertaken on the subject. Nor is there any publication on the information needs of couples in relationships with violence, (physical or non-physical). It explores the nature of, causes of and the prevention of violence, paying particular attention to the non-physical aspects. So, three years after completion of the original research, this is still a unique document in the violence business, an industry where over-duplication and conformity carries the swing.

Questionnaire Exercise

You can check whether your perception of or attitude to violence can, in any way, be affected by the information in this book by answering the questionnaire starting on page 177. First fill it in before reading the book and then compare the difference after reading (you can use page 191, the blank page at the end, to make notes). If you please, send me a copy of the results, care of Sukisa Publications at the publisher's address (see page ii). Unless you state categorically that you do want to be identified in future publications, your anonymity will be strictly protected.

S.R.

Contents

PART I

Introduction

Several years ago I saw a male friend of mine crying hysterically because of some problems he had with his female partner which resulted in him spending the night in jail. He wasn't crying because of his police-cell experience, he was crying he said, because he could not take any more of her terrorism. He was angry he said, because they put the wrong person in jail. When I later saw the damage he had done to her face, I could not agree with him. I wondered what he was talking about. There was nothing wrong with him but she had a busted mouth and a swollen face, yet he was saying she should have been locked up. The man was crazy, I thought.

Looking at my own personal experiences before and since then, (which I have chosen to relate in the first person for best effect), have led me to believe that a person can be terribly, and in some cases fatally, violated and brutalised by another person half her or his size without ever being *physically* assaulted by the perpetrator.

For example, I know a woman who had been psychologically terrorised in a systematic manner for a period of nearly three years by her partner, a softly spoken but short-tempered, small man. One night, after being "spoken to" by him, without any physical violence from him, she charged out of the house and deliberately ran straight into the road in front of an oncoming car.

Another example is of a man who, ordinarily could be thought of as a strong, intelligent, level-headed person, but after several months of a particularly destructive series of verbal and psychological assaults from his partner, was reduced to a "snivelling wreck" as he described himself and even came to doubt his own sanity - a condition also experienced by myself and observed in others by the researchers Binney, Harkell and Nixon. They reported that "Some women had been verbally tormented and threatened, until they were confused about their own sanity."[1]

Over the years, however, I have noticed in the various media what appears to be a growing tendency to label the man in domestic violence cases as the violent partner because it is the woman who is usually, physically violated or injured.[2] That kind of sentiment is so pervasive that a statement such as, "the problem [of domestic violence] is more *accurately* described as the problem of *violent husbands*"[3] goes virtually unchallenged.

The anger generated in me by this observation was exacerbated by a recent television documentary on domestic violence. The presenter, a twelve-year practising barrister, said as a statement of fact, "domestic violence is carried out by men". This was backed up by a visual statement that, "Women account for all victims of marital assault"[4][their underline]. That was the last straw. My personal experience and my observation of other couples in problematic relationships, spoke very differently. I could not believe that what I saw throughout my life - mutually destructive relationships - was a unique distortion of reality. I felt the need then to conduct my own research into relationship violence, under controlled academic conditions just to see ...

---

[1] Binney,V., Harkell,G. and Nixon,J., *Leaving Violent Men: A Study of Refuges and Housing for Battered Women,* Womens Aid Federation (UK) 1981 p4

[2] Pahl,J., (editor), *Private Violence and Public Policy: The needs of battered women and the response of the public services,* Routledge and Kegan Paul, 1985

Binney,V., et al, 1981 ppii-vii

Borkowski,M., Murch,M. and Walker,V., *Marital Violence: The Community Response,* Tavistock Publications 1983 p51

[3] Pahl,J., 1985 p5

[4] Woodcraft,E.(presenter), Dobbs,R.(prod.) and Evans,B.(Dir.), *Do Families Need Fathers?* Maya Vision Productions for Channel 4, 3.12.1992

More recently, as this book neared completion, I attended the first ever conference of African[5] and Asian professional men and women on the subject of sexual abuse or what I would call sexual violence in the African community[6]. It focused squarely on the question of sexual violence against girls and young women. When one of the presenters, Jackie Holder, declared that "...the increase in Black male violence in our community has affected the kind of dialogue and *created* certain rifts amongst Black men and Black Women" and "Black men have been the main perpetrators of abuse in our community", it was enthusiastically accepted by the majority of those gathered. When that idea was finally challenged by one person who questioned the responsibility of women in violent relationships, it was strongly reconfirmed by another presenter, Eden Charles, one of those "New Man" types, as "just a fact" that in relationships between African men and African women, "most of the violence come from Black men".

Lennox Thomas, representing NAFSIYAT on the platform, an organisation which counsels mainly African and Asian clients, said "You can only hold that notion of both of us are responsible ... if you actually think that the relationship is equal and is based on an equal sense of social power and social responsibility, which I don't think is so." In other words, women cannot be equally responsible because of the unequal power relations in society.

Chinweizu makes more or less the same statement in his thought-provoking book "Anatomy of Female Power"[7] but essentially, from the opposite perspective. He says that

---

[5] For the benefit of this book, 'African' includes any person of African ancestry (usually called American, Black, British, Coloured, Negro, Jamaican, Nigerian, etc.) regardless where they were born or are currently domiciled.

[6] "Living and Working with Sexual Abuse in the Black Community: a one day conference for Black men and Black women Professionals" organised by Pat Agana of Training for Life (*see Appendix A for contact*).

[7] Chinweizu, *Anatomy of Female Power: a Masculinist dissection of Matriarchy*, PERO Press, 1990

"feminist propaganda has sought to persuade the world that women are powerless in society and that men are natural oppressors of women"[8]but contrary to popular belief and misinformation, "in human society, it is not male power but female power which is supreme".[9]

This book is not part of an argument about which gender/sex is the strongest, the weakest, the most oppressed, most oppressive, who is more callous or sensitive, most or least powerful or destructive in a relationship; it is not about apportioning blame between men and women nor is it about 'paying back' or 'getting even'; it is not about making meaningless excuses or offering irrelevant, sanctimonious apologies for irresponsible and unacceptable behaviour.

This book is about harmony, balance, honesty, communication, understanding, responsibility and power. It is part of a search for solutions to the problem of violence in relationships, the kind of problems we all face each and every day of our lives. I believe that men and women, whenever we come together, are supposed to be partners in this process of life. In order for this life to be healthy and free of violence, it requires balance, and we can only have balance in a state of equilibrium.

Steinmetz's statement in 1973 that "women are as likely to select physical violence to resolve marital conflicts as are men",[10] is one of the few pronouncements which tend to contradict most of the statements made by her contemporaries. But, judging by the bibliographic references they cite,

---

[8] Chinweizu, Page 9

[9] Chinweizu, Page 11

[10] Steinmetz,S.K., 'Wife Beating, Husband Beating - A comparison of the use of Physical Violence Between Spouses to Resolve Marital Fights', University of Delaware, p68 in Roy,M., (Ed.) *Battered Women: A Psychological Study of Domestic Violence,* Von Nostrand Reinhold, New York 1977 pp63-72 [She was citing a seminar paper presented to the annual meeting of the American Sociological Association in 1973 by Straus,M.A., Gelles,R. and Steinmetz,S.K. entitled "Theories, Methods and Controversies in the Study of Violence Between Family Members"

and according to Roy,[11] they all made use of some of the same sources of information, yet arrived at almost contradictory conclusions. I wanted to find out why. Why was there, and still is, such a united voice, singing what I believed then to be an entirely untrue song?

As a violent person myself, the product of a violent society, I wanted to find out what caused me to violate my partners and what I could do about it; as a victim of violence in my adult relationships, casualty in another way of a violent society, I wanted to understand what caused my partners to violate me and again, what I could do to prevent it in future.

According to Zelda West-Meads of Relate,[12] one of Britain's largest marriage guidance organisations, the major cause of interpersonal relationship breakdowns, is the inability of couples to communicate or talk through their differences,[13] a condition which is compounded by the lack of relevant information. I believe that communication and information are the keys to resolving social problems so I set out to see what kind of information is available to people on the issue of interpersonal non-physical violence and how it is communicated to us, if at all.

---

[11] Roy,M., (Ed.) *Battered Women: A Psychological Study of Domestic Violence,* Von Nostrand Reinhold, New York 1977 pxi

[12] Relate, (*see Appendix A for contact*)

[13] Ajoni,A., *The Relationship Business,* Candid Books 1989 p8

Chapter One

The Questions

If the inability to communicate is the major cause of relationship breakdowns, could lack of communication also be a contributory factor in relationship violence? - particularly when it is considered that not all relationships which include violence actually break down? How much communication can be expected to take place between couples who are actually in the process of destroying each other and their relationship? What role does information or the lack of it play, if any, in the lives of couples involved in violent relationships?

What is the definition of the term "violence" and what is its true nature? Is it only physical, as most commentators would have us believe,[14] or is it, as the research will try to show, more generally non-physical violation, outrage, injury, (where injury is defined as: "any wrong or damage done to a man's [or woman's] person, rights, reputation or goods"[15]) as defined by some other commentators?.

What information do the researchers into violence between couples impart to their readers about the nature of violence and the relationship between physical and non-physical violence? Why is it, as stated by Stets that: "... surprisingly little research has examined verbal aggression, especially its relationship to physical aggression."[16] (*see Definitions*) How do the public in general and in particular those who have been involved in relationships with violence define violence? Do they

[14] Griffiths,G. & Davies,A., *Making Fathers Pay*, Public Eye BBC 2 TV 1990

[15] Wood,J., ed. *Nuttall's Standard Dictionary of the English Language*, Warne & co.1893

[16] Stets,J.E., 'Verbal and Physical Aggression in Marriage', *Journal of Marriage and the Family*, v52 n2 , May 1990 p501-14

recognise non-physical assault, repression, denial of rights, psychological, political, cultural, social and spiritual subversion, unwelcome sexual or emotional intervention, oppression and alienation of another person or persons as violence? What role do the media play in the public image of the nature of violence?

What is the attitude of professionals and carers to relationship violence in its broadest sense? How do they communicate this to their clients? Do they, in informing their clients, distinguish between physical violence and all the other non-physical aspects of violence? What tactics do they employ in satisfying the information needs of their clients? How do they deal with or treat cases where non-physical violence seems to be prevalent?

What does the law have to say about relationship violence; what kind of messages does it send in terms of prohibitions and/or penalties, to someone who is experiencing physical or non-physical violence in their relationship? The objective has been to answer all these questions and, hopefully, they will have been answered satisfactorily within the limitations of the accessible resources and human co-operation.

There are other important questions which could not, reasonably, be expected to be fully answered within the limitations of this project. They include: what effect does the cultural backgrounds of the individuals and the culture of their immediate environment have on their information gathering ability and the quality of information they are able to access? How would better, more truthful education about the values of different cultures temper the result? What role, if any, does the quality and type of information about colour/racial differences play in a mixed relationship in determining violence or harmony between them? what effect does the knowledge or ignorance of their relative histories have on the relationship?.

What would be the role of the information professionals in relation to the carers? In the context of a violent relationship what effect does non-violence have; does it help to prevent more violence or does it encourage more violence. Though fleeting, some light will be shed on these questions but broader, more in-depth research needs to be undertaken on the subject of violence from the perspective of this book in order for the above questions to be more fully answered.

Definitions

Violence

used to be defined as "physical force; strength of action or motion; vehemence; fierceness; highly excited feeling; *outrage; crime of any kind; injury; rape;*"[17] but more and more, violence is being seen only as the use or exercise of physical force.[18]

There can really be nothing wrong with violence at all, if it is defined merely as "physical force" or "the use of physical force". The use of physical force is not in itself harmful, in fact, as any scientist or physics professor will tell you, physical force is a necessary ingredient in almost every area of life including industry, mining, sports, even chewing. I can't accept that the physical force required to operate a piece of industrial machinery or the physical force generated by it, is violence; nor do I see the physical force exerted in eating a meal or engaging in sexual intercourse as violence.

Another definition of violence, though sticking firmly with the physical, qualifies the statement to read: "the exercise of physical force so as to inflict injury on or damage to persons

---

[17] Wood,J., ed. ibid.

[18] Borkowski,M., et al, 1983 p8

or property; action or conduct characterised by this"[19] That definition suggests that violence has a negative, undesirable characteristic and is not a neutral "physical force"

In this society, a violent society,[20] where physical force is sometimes used, or is threatened to be used, by the state as a means of establishing a semblance of order and of enforcing or imposing laws, violence has come to be defined as the "unlawful" or *illegal* use of physical force.[21] A state of affairs which makes the "lawful" use of physical force, even where it tends "to inflict injury on or damage to persons or property" justifiable in the eyes of the state and hence "non-violent".

For example, it is pronounced "lawful" therefore not violence, when agents of a government, such as the United States government, assassinate scores of unarmed Africans in their beds because they happen to be members of the Black Panther Party, an organisation they disapproved of; or agents of the British government, assassinate in cold blood, again without warning, unarmed individuals in a foreign land because they are members of a so-called "terrorist" organisation, the IRA. These are violent acts which are not seen as violent by the state because even though they are intended to be terminally destructive they are performed on behalf of the state, therefore lawful, therefore not violent.

There is a broader, earlier definition (1715), which goes outside the 'physical force' and 'lawful' confines with: "Undue constraint applied to some natural process, habit, etc."[22] This definition, though it only qualifies the amount or degree of constraint or repression to a non-specific "undue" level, never the less tends, to favour more the non-physical aspects of violence than the physical.

---

[19] *The Shorter Oxford English Dictionary,* Oxford University Press 1983.

[20] Hess,P., *Culture of Violence: The Foundation of White America on Slavery and Genocide: a call for White solidarity with Black Power*, Burning Spear Publications, 1991

[21] *Collins Concise Dictionary Plus,* William Collins 1989

[22] *The Shorter Oxford English Dictionary,* Oxford University Press 1983.

This aspect of interpersonal relationships where no physical force is used - in some instances no force at all in the accepted sense of the word, is used - but one party is harmed, injured, disadvantaged, or infringed upon etc. by the wilful, deliberate actions of another, is called non-physical violence, which is the major focus of this work.

For the benefit of this book, violence is defined as:

any act which violates;

where violate, coming from the same Latin root as violence which signifies power, force or strength, is defined as: to transgress; to infringe; to injure; to disturb; to break; to offend; to do violence to.

In other words:

> **violence is any act, whether covert or overt, which is intended to, designed to or calculated to cause pain, injury, discomfort, disadvantage to or otherwise harm or destroy, transgress or infringe on a person or persons;**

this includes every form of **physical** assault from "minor" physical assault like a slap or shove to very serious physical assaults such as rape, injury with weapons, imprisonment or the ultimate extreme of killing with torture (with or without weapons), and the various forms of **non-physical** assault such as verbal abuse, repression, constraint, infringement or denial of rights, psychological, sexual, political, cultural, social and spiritual subversion, oppression and alienation of a person or persons.

In this context violence will be used synonymously and interchangeably with violation

Aggression

is defined by Stets[23] as synonymous with violence as it is used in family violence research[24] and verbal aggression is synonymous with "psychological aggression",[25] "emotional abuse" or "psychological maltreatment"[26] or non-physical violence.

Aggression is also defined by Baron[27] as "any form of behaviour directed toward the goal of harming or injuring another living being who is motivated to avoid such treatment." And if the victim is not *motivated* to such avoidance?

Relationship,

for the purpose of this project, is defined as the condition which exists between two or more people interacting with each other as individuals or as distinguishable entities.

Interpersonal Relationship

is defined as a union of two or more people relating on a "romantic" and/or emotional level as friends, lovers, partners, spouses, soul mates, and/or companions.

Responsibility

is defined as the state or position of being responsible[28]

Responsible

is defined by Collins as:

1. having control or authority (over)

---

[23] Stets,J.E., May 1990 p502

[24] Gelles,R.J. and Straus,M.A., Determinants of Violence in the Family: Toward a theoretical integration in Wesley R. Burr, Rueben Hill, F. Ivan Nye, and Ira L. Reiss (eds.), *Contemporary Theories About the Family* (Vol.1) New York: Free Press 1979 pp549-581

[25] Mason,A. and Blankenship,V., "Power and Affiliation Motivation, Stress, and Abuse in Intimate Relationships." *Journal of Personality and Social Psychology* 52: 203-210 1987

[26] Garbino,J., Guttman,E. and Seeley,J., *The Psychologically Battered Child,* San Francisco: Josey-Bass 1986

[27] Baron,R.A., *Human Aggression,* Plenum 1977, p7

[28] *Collins Concise Dictionary Plus,* William Collins 1989

2. being accountable for one's own actions and decisions

3. involving decisions and accountability

4. being the agent or cause of some action

5. able to take rational decisions without supervision; accountable for one's own actions

6. able to meet financial obligations; of sound credit.[29]

In this book **responsible** is synonymous with **accountable**. Accountable for your own actions; accountable for the consequence of those actions, even where the consequences cannot be foreseen; accountable to yourself and those with whom you interact, for the way you behave (or not behave) in such interaction, even where the behaviour appears to be triggered, manipulated or caused by those other people.

For the benefit of this book being responsible for someone does not mean having "control of or authority" over or ownership of that person, it means being accountable (in conjunction with the person), for that person's welfare not for their actions. So, if you are responsible for someone, you should be able to say or show what you are doing or have done, that is intended to benefit or be in the interest of the person. For example, what you are doing to help them avoid violence.

Responsible does not mean blameable or creditable or as Collins says: "being the agent or *cause* of some action". We are accountable for everything we do and their consequences but we are not accountable for someone else's action, even where they are merely reacting to something we said or did. They are accountable for their own actions. Responsibility is not synonymous with blame or credit.

---

[29] *Collins Concise Dictionary Plus*, William Collins 1989

Responsibility is not something which can be given to you by someone else who decides that you are "able to take *rational* action without supervision"; your responsibility for yourself and your actions may well be recognised or not recognised by other people but their sanction is not what determines whether you are responsible or not. You are the only person who can determine whether you can or can not make decisions or take actions, regardless whether anyone else thinks they are rational or irrational or whether you should be supervised or not because whatever actions you take you are accountable to yourself for.

So for the benefit of this book **responsibility** is defined as:

> **the state of being *accountable to yourself* and to those with whom you interact, *for your own actions* and the consequences of those actions.**

Hypothesis

I intend to show that contrary to popular belief, violence in relationships is not just physical assault committed by men on women; that violence as previously defined above, happens in all relationships (heterosexual or homosexual) where there are problems, even where the problems are experienced or noticed by only one partner; that both parties, men and women are equally and totally responsible for what happens in the relationship, the best as well as the worst aspects, including violence.

I will show that women are also psychologically, emotionally, spiritually and socially violated by men more often and sometimes more seriously, than physically; women also violate men on <u>all</u> those levels to more or less the same degree; and both men and women violate children most of the time with even more serious consequences because those same children are the ones who are expected to produce better children when they grow into adults.

Violence is the negative manifestation of a struggle or a search for power when the individual's need to fulfil her or his natural desire for power over self[30] is diverted, through social programming, into a quest to exercise power over others. The struggle is usually initiated within the individual person when he or she comes into contact with another person who resists in any way her or his attempts to control or exercise power over that person. Of course, apparent lack of resistance on the part of the victim does not mean that violence is not being committed; there could be many reasons why the violated person does not appear to resist, including the fact that they may believe it is in their best interest not to resist; it may be that they have been swindled or tricked by a politician or some other kind of crook into believing that their interest is best served if they surrender to surrogacy.

Resistance or conflict may be due to the fact that the other person is also seeking to control and manipulate as a means of satisfying their own innate desire for power over self; or it may be that they have gone through or are going through a process of deprogramming which does not allow them to accommodate or condone their own enslavement or the oppression of others. Regardless what the reasons are for the resistance, such a reaction is experienced by the would-be controller as a threat or an attack upon her or him and is met with greater violence. And so the cycle of violence escalates. But violence is not caused by the exercise of power over self, it is caused mainly by the quest for power over others.

Some commentators, such as Robert J. Powers,[31] see the use of violence in the quest for power over others in a

---

[30] R.,S., "Leadership and Self-determination" in *Global Africa Pocket News*, Vol.1, #6 June '94
[31] Powers,R.J., In *Violent Transactions*, Basil Blackwell, 1986

relationship as constructive rather than destructive because it does not have as its primary aim harming the victim, even if it is harmful. He says, in his criticism of another writer, Baron's definition (*see Definitions*) of aggression: "For example, an individual may desire greater power and control in a relationship and may become verbally insulting or physically abusive in an effort to gain greater influence". How could abusing or otherwise violating someone to gain control of them or greater influence over them ever be constructive? For whom is it constructive? When we all come to recognise our own absolute powers of self-determination, there will be no basis for violence of any kind in relationships.

The underlying cause of violence is a perceived lack of power. "That's absolute nonsense!" I hear you say, "Men have all the power and they are the violent ones." I don't expect you to, nor ask you to, agree with me, just listen to (read) what I say and try to understand, that is all I ask. The view that the user of violence has essentially a problematic relationship with their own power and their environment is also supported by Frances Cress-Welsing in her statement that the liberal - careless - destructive use of violence by Europeans[32] in their quest for dominance over other peoples, particularly African people, is due to a deep-rooted inferiority complex.[33] Similarly, Dr. John Henrik Clarke states that: "Many of these Europeans felt called upon to make non-Europeans feel inferior so that they could convince themselves that they were superior"[34]

It will be shown that because of the deliberate dissemination of erroneous and misleading information and the unavailability of relevant information in the media, from most

---

[32] For the benefit of this essay, European includes any person of European ancestry (usually called white or Caucasian) regardless where they were born or are currently domiciled.

[33] Cress-Welsing,F., *The Cress Theory of Color-Confrontation and RACISM (White Supremacy): (a Psycho-Genetic Theory and World Outlook)*, C-R Publishers 1970

[34] in his introduction to the 1990 edition of *The Iceman Inheritance* by Michael Bradley

researchers[35] and from some professionals on the nature, causes and prevention of relationship violence, false beliefs and prejudicial attitudes are being fostered in the minds of couples and individuals, thereby increasing rather than decreasing the risk of further and greater incidence of violence, both physical and non-physical, between them.

In other words, people are being misinformed into believing that they are either powerless -impotent - on the one hand because of some external factor such as "the system", history, race/religion or biological/gender factor such as being a woman or Aboriginal. On the other hand, they may be led to believe that they are all-powerful - omnipotent - because they have some natural, inherent power over other people for the same reasons. Neither of which is true. **None of us is powerless.** Whatever power anybody seems to have over us is entirely by our consent. The exercise of their power depends on our concession and because that consent can be withdrawn at any moment, **nobody** can have absolute power over us.[36]

People accept powerlessness. They accept it when they think that certain things happen in their relationships because of some inherent defect in themselves or because of some biologically determined superior or inferior qualities in their partners. When they believe that their lack of power is due entirely to factors beyond their control such as historical inheritance, gender difference or "racial" background or any number of predetermined factors, they are also accepting powerlessness, thereby relinquishing their responsibility for determining what happens between them - good or bad.

---

[35] Stets,J.E., May 1990,
Borkowski,M., et al, 1983,
Griffiths,G. & Davies,A., 1990,
Binney,V., et al, 1981,
Woodcraft,E., Dobbs,R. and Evans,B., 3.12.1992 .

[36] R,S., *The Human Value,* Sukisa Publications, 1987 p4

We are all responsible for ourselves. We are responsible for everything we do and we are responsible for the consequence of everything we do. I must stress that this does not mean that you alone are responsible, it means that you are equally responsible with all who you interact for the result of that interaction.

Our responsibility and power in a relationship and hence our value in the relationship is determined by the mere fact of being in the relationship. A relationship can be likened to a circle and our position as a partner in any relationship can be likened to that of any section of a circle. Imagine a circle of atoms whose outline is the thickness of one atom, spanning the circumference of the Earth. Every single atom in that circle is as important as every other in relation to the circle. In fact each atom is as important to the maintenance of that circle as the sum total of all the other atoms because if just one atom is removed, the result would be a very long symmetrically curved line, there would no longer be a circle.

Similarly, in a relationship between a man and a woman, the relationship, which is itself a quite separate entity, depends for its existence on the involvement of both its particles. Both parties are of equal value to the maintenance or the destruction of the relationship; they therefore command equal power and bear equal responsibility for what happens in the relationship. This is illustrated more clearly in the process of procreation where, regardless how little or how great either partner's contribution may appear to be, both are of equal value to the resultant creation and hence have equal responsibility for that entity. This is what is meant by the "duality of the one" concept, where two entities (man and woman) come together and become one (couple) while at the same time remaining separate, complete, identifiable and self-determinate individuals capable of relating to a multitude of other entities.

Essentially, we are either responsible for everything we do every second of our lives - and its possible consequences - even being in the "wrong" place at the "wrong" time and ending up murdered, raped or robbed because we could have done something else or been somewhere else. Or we are not at all responsible for anything we do; we can disclaim responsibility for even the most horrific acts, where we spend a long time consciously plotting and planning, on the grounds that society, psychology, biology, God or the Devil made us do it.

Because life is a web of interrelated interactions, we can always find something - anything - leading up to the incident, which we can use as the excuse to relinquish responsibility for or find justification for our actions. For example some people now believe that the cause of all their problems in their lives is the way they were delivered at birth.[37] Of course, the way a person is delivered at birth must have an effect on who they are and what they turn out to be, just as being in a smoke-filled room or meeting someone for 10 minutes once in your life will also have an effect. But would it be fair to say that either the meeting or the cigarette smoke is the cause of you having a knock-down-drag-out fight with your partner thirty years later?

A meets B; A gives B a gift (a mango or a £50,000 diamond ring). They are both happy. Is B responsible for what happened there, for them being happy together? Yes, of course. B is responsible for her or his interaction with A, which resulted in the presentation of a gift and their particular action or reaction in receipt of the present.

A attacks B. The attacker A, is clearly responsible for the act of stabbing, shooting, poisoning, cursing or whatever means was used to assault B. The immediate consequence is

---

[37] Oprah Winfrey show, Channel 4 TV, 13.10.1994

that B is injured and A is responsible for that. B is responsible for being involved in her or his injury, not necessarily for the injury but for the process of interaction which resulted in the injury.

You say: "that is OK if it is an argument between two people but what about the child who is killed, raped or assaulted by an adult, how could he or she be responsible in any way?" That is a question which needs to be addressed fully in another book but I will try to introduce the concept here in a later chapter.

Being unaware of what we are doing does not diminish our responsibility for our actions, nor does lack of awareness of the possible consequences absolve us from suffering or enjoying the consequence. Ignorance can help to reduce the degree to which we are credited or blamed for the act and its consequence but it can have no effect on the question of our responsibility for ourselves, our actions and the consequences of those actions.

Violence flourishes in an environment of ignorance. Ignorance of self is probably the most unfavourable state any person or group of human beings can find themselves in. If "knowledge of self is the key to life"[38] then lack of knowledge of self is the door to death. Any person or group of people who induces ignorance, prevents another person or group of people from acquiring knowledge, prevents them from being informed or is deliberately misinforming them, is committing an act of violence.

It is only when the truth about self-empowerment, for both men and women, and the responsibility that goes with it, is told, heard, understood and accepted as part of the information transfer process, will the true definition of violence be faced. Then the courage will be found to identify its causes

[38] Motto at the front page of ***Global Africa Pocket News*** magazine which is an interpretation of the words inscribed by the Africans in the temples in Egypt.

and the facility will be applied to prevent its occurrence. We cannot prevent violence with lies because the lie is just another form of violence - non-physical violence. To be well informed is to be empowered.

Aims and Objectives

In today's world any relationship which does not feature physical violence such as grabbing, gouging, pushing, punching, kicking, stabbing or shooting is said to be peaceful or "non-violent". There have been instances where people have committed or attempted to commit suicide, citing the terror of life in apparently "non-violent" relationships as the cause.

Even societies where government agents regularly torture or kill their fellow citizens under the guise of defending law and order, are referred to as "peaceful" or "non-violent" societies.

Aims

The overall aim of this research is to give a deeper understanding of the information needs of people (couples in particular) who are involved in relationships which include violence, both physical and non-physical. To review the quality and quantity of relevant information available to them on the nature, causes and prevention of violence in relationships, including "non-violent" relationships where only the absence of physical violence is apparent.

Objectives

These overall aims can be broken down into the following, more specific objectives:

a) to investigate the quality and quantity of information available to and/or imparted to couples on the nature of violence i.e. the different ways in which they may violate each other paying particular attention to the non-physical (psychological, emotional, social and spiritual) aspects of violence because although a great deal of research has been done on physical violence, hardly any has looked at non-physical violence to the same degree[39]

b) to evaluate the accessibility of relevant information, e.g. "...open and safe communication about sexual matters" and power relations,[40] to couples who are experiencing difficulties in relating to each other harmoniously

c) to evaluate the quality and quantity of information available to couples on the causes of and possible means of preventing violence in interpersonal relationships, through information professionals and information systems

d) to evaluate the level and quality of communication between couples who are involved in violent interpersonal relationships

e) to investigate how information on relationship violence is portrayed by the media to the public in general

---

[39] Stets,J.E., May 1990 p501

[40] Rodgerson,G. and Wilson,E., (eds.) *Pornography and Feminism: The Case Against Censorship,* Feminists Against Censorship/Lawrence and Wishart, 1991 p15

f) to investigate the role of ethnic and cultural differences in violent relationships

g) to evaluate what effect information or lack of information on ethnic and cultural differences have on the creation or prevention of violence

h) to evaluate the quality and quantity of information available from professionals in the field, such as counsellors, carers and lawyers on the nature and causes of violence in interpersonal relationships

i) to produce, after analysis of the data collected, a report (this book) on the information needs of couples and some of the possible causes of and probable solutions to the problem of interpersonal relationship violence.

Purpose

"Why publish yet another book on domestic violence?" I hear you ask. It is readily accepted that there are hundreds of books on the subject of domestic violence but most of them deal primarily with the physical aspects of violence, with one party, usually the female, as the victim and the other party as the perpetrator. There appears to be great reluctance to accept that in any relationship both parties can be victims and both can be violators.

It seems that in order for most people to have a clear picture of who the victim is there must be a clear picture of who or where the violator is. For this reason researchers have published the evidence that in many cases show neither the violence nor the pain was one-sided but never the less come to the traditional conclusion that violence in relationships is male on female physical assault. Anyone who suggests that violence in a relationship could be mutual or that the victim could also be the criminal is shouted down in a chorus.

In response to the suggestion that women are equally responsible for what happens in their relationships, Sister Namonyah, an African healer who deals mainly with battered women, said: "Until we get to a place where we are truly empowered as a people and dealing with internalised racism in getting that out of our lives and removing the chains of mental slavery (because we are still dealing with mental slavery which is very devastating and dysfunctional for us as a people), until we deal with that kind of spiritual self-empowerment it is a very dangerous thing to say that people are responsible for abuse, on many different levels."[41] It is indeed "dangerous" to suggest that we are responsible for what happens in our relationships because if we come to believe that, we would then find ourselves having to do something about them ourselves.

On the other hand, not all women subscribe to the idea of female irresponsibility. Sister Nzinga Assata, for example, says: "We as sisters, have equal responsibility for our self-development and for what happens to us. We must stop being victims and allowing all sorts of destructive things to happen to us and take our destiny in our hands. We are each accountable for ourselves and we are just as much to blame as men for the situation that we are in."[42]It could hardly be better expressed. If only more people were willing to take responsibility for their interaction...

The purpose of this research is:

a) in consideration of the paucity of relevant information available in the field,[43]to provide an

[41] Speaking from the floor at the Training for Life, Sexual Abuse conference, London, 1994.

[42] Speaking from the floor at a conference of the African United Action Front in London, 1994.

alternative view of violent relationships from the one which says that relationship violence is physical assault, it is a one-way street and it can be prevented from recurring by the punishment of one of the partners, usually the man, or the temporary or permanent separation of the parties involved.

b) To provide easier access to more and better information for people, as to how and why they are or have been violating their partners or are being or have been violated. By publishing this book we would hope to encourage better, more professional and less biased personal advice and counselling,[44] better information in the form of books, pamphlets, leaflets, magazine articles, TV and radio programs with clear suggestions or instructions as to what can be done to reverse or curtail the process of escalating violence.

c) to assist professionals where both covert and overt violence, is utilised by one or both partners as the final arbiter. To quote but one research team: "The training programmes of social, medical and legal agencies should include the topic of domestic violence - its scope, severity and solutions."[45]

d) to inspire and incite debate on the subject of relationship violence.

---

[43] Stets,J.E., May 1990 p501

[44] Allam,F., *Unspeakable Acts,* Dir. L.Jackson, BBC community Programme Unit, BBC2 April 1993.

[45] Binney,V., et al, 1981pix

e) finally, and probably most importantly, in a world where the tendency is to see non-physical violence as "normal" acceptable behaviour, it is also intended to help prevent the escalation of violence in relationships where there is no physical violence.

Such relationships may be considered to be non-violent, due to the prevailing sentiment that "violence" means physical assault. By providing better, less biased information on the *nature* of interpersonal relationship violence, and the seriousness and destructiveness of non-physical relationship violence,[46] we hope to be able to help people to eliminate violence of all kinds from their lives on every level.

Scope

The scope of this study was potentially very broad-based in the sense that the outreach could have included all adults of both sexes, of every cultural, social, religious, economic and occupational backgrounds, who had had the experience of a personal relationship where there had been violence of any kind. Practical restrictions such as lack of resources and demographic constraints dictated a much narrower investigation.

In practice the outreach was restricted to the distribution of a questionnaire (*see appendix F*) on the university campus, at a few counselling organisations and through personal contact with individuals in a random manner (*see Methodology*) and interviews with some of the people who had completed and returned

[46] Binney, V., et al, 1981 pp4-5

their questionnaires and who indicated that they would agree to be interviewed (*see Case Stories*).

The study also focused on the role of professionals who deal with relationship problems and interpersonal violence by looking at the information available on the subject. This included seeking information by way of interviews with representatives from organisations such as London Marriage Guidance (Relate), Everyman Centre, Camden Black Sisters, Women Against Rape, etc., as well as trying to interview representatives from the legal profession. I say "trying" to interview because the problems encountered in the attempt to secure any kind of on-the-record comment from the legal profession dealing with this subject was indeed a trying experience.

Case Stories

The following case histories are based on some of the interviews with volunteers and some answers to questions from the questionnaire (*see Appendix F*). Of course, you must remember that these stories are all very short accounts of what must have been long and very complex relationships and although I would not want to cast aspersions on the honesty and integrity of any of my subjects (there is nothing to suggest that anything any one of them said was a lie), they are all never the less one-sided, unverifiable accounts and must be taken as such.

For smoothness of flow, the first-person narrative style is used here instead of the question and answer style. Each one of the seven interviews reproduced in part here has been chosen because it has a particular message which I want to relay to you dear reader. There were many similarities between the answers to identical and very similar questions as well as unique answers to unique questions.

Rather than just print everything that was said I chose to include those parts which would allow the narrative to flow easily without too much repetition. Might I suggest a look at the questionnaire and the Sample Questions to Volunteers (*Appendix D*) before reading the stories, they may help you to get a clearer understanding of the relevance of some of the statements.

If you have not yet done so, now might be a good time to fill in a copy of the questionnaire yourself to test your own experience and perception of violence.

All the names of those interviewed have been changed to protect the volunteers, their families and friends, who may be adversely affected by any negative publicity which may be generated by the publication of this book if they were identified.

Since the original research was completed many people hearing of the project have shown an interest in helping. I have since interviewed and chatted with a few of them but their contributions mainly confirm and strengthen my findings rather than shine any new or different lights on the subject of relationship violence.

Fiona

Fiona is a young European librarian who was involved in a violent, "secret" relationship with an Asian student. Even though she agreed to it at the beginning and thought it would be in her interest professionally, she felt the secrecy about their relationship was imposed on her. And though she knew from the outset that he intended to return home at the completion of his studies without her, she felt that the temporary nature of their relationship was also imposed on her; she felt restricted. Fiona says:

"Well, it was a private relationship and nobody was supposed to know about it. I came to know him through my work. I work in the library and he was a student who came to the library. He felt inhibited [about the involvement] amongst his friends where he lived. He shared a house with other students who were all male. He is Asian and most of the people he shared his house with were also Asian or Oriental and I think this had something to do with the desire for secrecy.

"Because of my work I didn't want it to be widely known either. Of course I told a friend of mine about it in confidence and she promised not to tell anybody - but I think she did. There were repercussions. He made more of a fuss about it than I did.

"I know this sounds illogical but I think sometimes people do apologise for what they haven't done when they are made to, especially by somebody they feel very close to. I didn't do anything to harm him but he thought that I had. He was believing things that were completely untrue. It was almost to the point in the end of some form of paranoia or some sort of personality abnormality. So I was saying that I was sorry to have made him feel like this but I hadn't done anything to harm him at all.

"You see he misinterpreted things very wildly - way out. I think part of the misinterpretation - perhaps on both sides - was perhaps cross-cultural misunderstandings, yes, that could be part of it. And also cultural differences and differences in background.

"I think that people could have warned me about the strangeness of his behaviour and his various instabilities, his strange ideas about things.

Cause of Violence

"I think the cause of violence was, apart from cultural differences, that he was suffering very badly and this was really a case of historical cause and effect. He has had quite an unhappy childhood and he had been the victim of child abuse, and I think it's affected his behaviour emotionally and in other ways.

Communication

"I think it certainly would have helped to have had enhanced communication but I don't think that it would have held all the answers in this case really. I think there were more disturbing things behind this that I don't think could have been sorted out by talking - not talking between us anyway. I think how people are treated as children can very largely determine how they behave in relationships in later life. In many ways I think I was very naive about this relationship.

Future Prospects

"Sadly, I feel that I will never be able to have a successful relationship with this person anymore. I still have good feelings for this person but I think that it would be impossible for everything to be all right. He has a special place in my memory and I'd like to keep the good side of this in my mind. I don't feel angry with him I just feel very sad and I hope that he can get better because I think that he is a little bit disturbed in his mind."

Abeo

Abeo is a 25 year old African student with a European father. She confused a relationship which she terminated after being physically assaulted, with her then current involvement where she was the only person using physical violence. She declared herself to be the perpetrator of violence in her relationship but found that there were other violations happening outside of the physical. She spoke of her current boyfriend who she believed used sex as a weapon but had never hit her except for "just a slap".

Nature of Violence

"I wouldn't say that he has been violent towards me. I would obviously assume that violence is physical violence. That's what I would say but if somebody tried to explain to me other forms, fair enough but I haven't got that in my head.

"In this relationship the violations are not physical as punches and things like that, they're more like he'll say he doesn't feel like it... that's his way. I'm not really violent myself, anyway, neither of us is violent. He's not physically violent at all - no."

In referring to her questionnaire answers where she said he retaliated verbally and physically to her physical and verbal abuses, she said: "Probably *just* a slap".

Later in the interview she tried to put the record straight: "I don't believe that I just said that, cause he hasn't hit me. So that must have been the other guy. He's never hit me. He's only slapped me once when I was drunk, it wasn't being malicious, he was just trying to wake me up kind of thing.

Cause of Violence

"I would say the cause of violence was all around sex, probably. I mean issues about sex. For example, if I'm not happy I would be abusive toward him and if I wanted to discuss an open relationship he would be abusive back - verbally abusive. Sometimes we resolved our problems by just having sex.

Communication

"On paper Abeo indicated her partner's inability to communicate as a cause of the difficulties they had in communicating sometimes but in interview she said: "I think we do communicate a lot. It's a very honest relationship and I think that's probably why it's still going. Cause if we have problems, I know me, definitely if I'm not happy with something -

discuss it straight away, it's not something that's kept quiet and hope it will change. Talk about it, definitely.

Future Prospects

"I think these S & M [Sadism and Masochism] people should be able to do what they like to each other in private. But if someone is getting a raw deal and it's not a two way thing, then I think there should be somewhere where they can go to get help. For example if it's a woman there should be a refuge and laws maybe, that can punish the other person involved because a lot of the time they [the victims] are not going to be strong enough to take the actions."

Christine

Christine is an employed professional, a college lecturer. She stated in her answers to the questionnaire that she had never been involved in a relationship with violence but continued to expose one particular relationship which was fraught with problems and mutual abuse to the point of her seeking to take out an injunction against her ex-partner.

Nature of Violence

"Violence is a very, very broad term and the way I understood violence as in relationship violence is mainly physical assault - but also aggravated verbal assault. If you call somebody an 'arsehole' or a 'cunt', yeah? or if you tell somebody repeatedly 'you are a fucking piece of shit', yeah? I mean the occasional 'bloody hell! what are you doing?', that I wouldn't class as a verbal assault or a verbal put-down because a lot in a relationship depends on the situation. So I went for the safe definition. It is incredibly difficult to see, especially psychological, emotional violence because it is so intangible but it is very real.

"It was quite a harsh formulation, I felt, especially the 'injury, pain' and I had never intended that. Discomfort probably, yes but the others - definitely not an injury, I didn't intend to inflict pain on that person. I thought about that one for a long time actually. But isn't then every relationship violent? I would argue with your definition of assault. What is a verbal assault, where do you draw the line?

Cause of Violence

"The main cause of violence was "Alcohol. He drank a lot. I think it was mainly because he was a very unhappy person who had a lot of personal problems when he was a teenager. Also a lot of it was that he very much fitted into the male stereotype and he played along with that role and that caused much problems.

"I got in touch with a solicitor who specialises in relationship violence and I wanted to get an injunction because although we were already separated, that person was still doing things. But I couldn't get one." According to the information she presented, it appears as though she was given inappropriate advice by an incompetent.

Communication

"Lack of communication played a huge part in creating problems in our relationship. I would say something and the response would be completely the other way or not respond at all. When I said we had a problem and suggested we go and see a counsellor, I was called neurotic and mad but I didn't actually get an explanation why. There was complete breakdown in communication.

"Because the violence happened sporadically and there were what seemed good intervals, it was at first very difficult to spot the patterns. But in the end it was complete breakdown of communication.

Future Prospects

"It was a learning process. You can't predict people and how they will develop, but definitely I feel much more able to spot signals, warning signals.

"It is a right that there should be information available. Also, relationship violence is still not considered a major problem. I know the police are changing their attitude to 'domestic violence' as it is called but there is still a long way to go."

Patrick

Patrick is a young, unemployed, alcoholic who was convicted of assaulting his former girlfriend and had to undergo treatment as part of the condition of his sentence.

Violent Background

"I think we were both very, very similar in our views because we both had disastrous relationships beforehand. Right from when we left home I suppose we were very let down and we were very afraid of situations of being rejected. We were both very similar in that way.

"I had relationships with women that were very violent. I mean, I was stabbed in one relationship with a pair of scissors.

"I know that when I was younger I was sexually attacked and I suffered a form of post traumatic stress. The girl that I was with, I found out after a while had been sexually abused as a child by her own family. I don't know whether it was because she was mentally disturbed as a result or whether she was seriously emotionally disturbed, but I had been to see a psychiatrist that she was seeing and he had warned me about her that the moment she was starting to get very close to somebody she would get violent.

"When I stop to think about the violence, I was never really violent myself. I was very strongly tempted to be but part of me just never wanted to and I never believed it was the right thing to do. I grew up in a family that were basically all violent; my father was an alcoholic who was violent; my elder brother was violent towards me and younger brother occasionally snapped and got violent. And I was the one who stood there and took it all, partly because I think, I was afraid. More than anything, I was afraid. I was afraid of getting hurt myself and partly I was afraid of how much damage I might do. I just sort of resisted doing it.

Non-physical Violence

Psychological Pain

"Right from when I was a child, I would give my brothers something and five minutes later deny that I had given it to them and then take it back. So I was being very psychological about hurting. I was even warned when I was at school about my behaviour. I seemed to have an ability to spot somebody's weakness and pick on it and verbally abuse that situation. It wasn't very pleasant and I was warned very strongly about it at school.

"About ten years ago I changed my life. I was drinking and I was hanging around with the wrong kind of people." Patrick dropped all his old friends, took counselling, gave up drinking and met his current girlfriend. They have been "Sort of happy together ever since."

Communication

"When I look upon it now, to me it seems, all because there was no communication; my father didn't talk, nobody sort of really discussed any situation and if a discussion developed, logically, there would have been an argument.

"To be honest, when I think of that relationship, it was a disastrous relationship that went on and on, but it started off perfectly alright. For about three to six months we were talking and communicating, there didn't seem to be any problems. Looking towards the future everything looked wonderful as if it could be. We were talking about getting married and everything. Suddenly, she just veered off - no more conversation.

"She never did love me. In fact she was using me to get away from somebody else at the time. Rather than come to me and say well look it's over, she still wanted somewhere safe to be and to me it was just staying in that situation for the sake of staying there and there was no point in carrying on.

"By this time she had started playing the field, anyway, so she always seemed to have somewhere to go and disappear but she could always come back. She would disappear for two or three days and turn up 3 o'clock in the morning throwing something through the window. It was just completely chaotic. Because of what had happened to her I just don't think she was capable of loving anyone. She didn't have any insight into her problems at all. She would just become more and more violent and I found that she was extremely violent with other people and she was going out drinking and fighting.

Prison

"For injuring someone very badly she was imprisoned. Unfortunately she escaped from prison and turned up at my address. I ended up getting arrested (and getting 6 months probation) for harbouring her, which was a very unpleasant experience. While all that was going on she decided to get physically violent with me again. I lost my temper this time and decided to finish it and the only way I could deal with her - she didn't understand language at all anymore - was physically. I had a terrible situation where I couldn't really do anything. I was being threatened by her family that if I called the police in I'd be in trouble. I found that I was so distraught and couldn't find any other method of dealing with the situation. The end result is that I hit her one night when she picked up a plastic bottle we were having a drink from, obviously she thought it was glass and went to hit me over the head with it. I lost my temper and hit her and knocked her cold. Basically, that was it; the police were called, I got arrested. She went back to prison and that was the last I saw of her. She did turn up once afterwards, thinking she could carry on as if nothing happened when she got out of prison. I just told her to go away, and she realised I meant it. But it is really sad to end up in a situation where you are drawn into using physical violence yourself.

Cause of Violence

"If I drink I have a tendency to lose control of my thoughts and everything as a result of the drinking and I revert back to remembering all the violence. I get very, very angry and very depressed so if I start to drink it makes it far worse. I then lose touch with reality.

"I am in counselling now, trying to resolve all of that and it's very difficult. I've still got stuck inside me lots of the anger at the people that attacked me. I was furious with my father 'cause he was constantly beating us and I used to run away from home. Once when I ran away I went to Brighton and I was sexually abused. I blamed my father for that as well. I ended up really suffering as a result of that.

"When I was going to see Luke he was giving me a lot more information than the counsellor I have now. It's very difficult because with general counselling it's entirely up to me what I bring to the counsellor to deal with. I don't really know in the end what to do. I feel trapped sometimes; it's a really unpleasant feeling.

Future Prospects

"When I think about what has happened to me in my life I'm somehow coming to terms with it in the sense that I'm not so upset that it actually happened anymore. I'm sort of getting to the point where all the things that happened to me make me feel stronger in a way. And I can understand lots of other people that's been hurt and suffered as well. My whole feeling has been changed to wanting to do something where I can care for other people. I suppose what has happened to me is making me understand other people and wanting to do more to help other people as well.

"To me, the way I look at it, if I'd been in the same situation and maybe I hadn't been sexually attacked maybe I would never have got to the point of suffering enough to want to change; I may have decided to be violent instead.

"When I left school I remember wondering why I'd been taught maths, English and everything and not how to live in life. Not so much at school but at home as well, parents should have some counselling before they even have children."

Femi

Femi is a professional musician who spent a remarkably long time in a very violent and mutually destructive relationship.

"I spent fifteen years of my life in a power struggle with one of the most vicious, cowardly and megalomanic people I have ever known. I believe her objective was to own me and control my entire behaviour.

Why Me?

"I don't know why she chose me, with so many men willing to be owned and controlled by a woman in return for comfort, mothering and a facade of exercising male authority - I really don't know why she chose me, someone who she knew before we met as a champion of self-determination, a freedom fighter. Maybe she just thought I would be a good catch. I really don't know. It may be that she is more courageous than I give her credit for and she just thought I would make a good challenge. I don't know. All I know is, we both wanted the same thing: to own and control my life.

Attraction

"I know why I chose her. It was not her figure, she was just a short, fat, almost shapeless, light-skin girl, nothing special. Her face? She had one of the most beautiful, proud faces I had ever seen - especially her well formed lips and her majestic profile. But it wasn't that either. It was her mind - sharp, witty, versatile, intelligent, broad, perceptive, fertile, wicked sense of humour - which captivated me. Oh yes and she had a keen ear and good rhythm; she could use her body. Add to that a fantastic sexual performance and you have the perfect bait. And I was caught. We had some beautiful times.

Cause of Violence

"So what went wrong? What went wrong was that the truth started to come out. I told her at the very beginning - when we first met, that I was not a one-woman man. She pretended for a long time that it was OK with her. But it wasn't OK, she lied. And I think that was the beginning of all the violence between us. Superficially, it was her intense jealousy and my outright refusal to succumb to it. Deeper than that, I think we were essentially, two incompatible characters whose sensual and intellectual attraction overwhelmed reason and common sense, giving way to dishonesty with ourselves and each other.

"She lied to me from the very beginning and although I was always truthful with her, I also lied to myself - too often. The violence started with lies but I wouldn't say that was the *cause* of violence because lies are also acts of violence. I would say that the cause of violence between us was us, the two of us. The way we related to each other, our expectations, actions, reactions - everything *we* did in relation to each other was the cause of violence. Of course she would tell you - in fact she has said it many times - that the cause of violence and the perpetrator of all the violence was me. She said that I was the problem. But I don't accept that.

"We had great fun for a little while but when she got pregnant with our first daughter everything changed. At least her attitude changed, if not my behaviour. As far as she was concerned I had nothing else to do with my life except have sex. And if I was not with her I was screwing some other woman - or 'bitch' as she called them.

History of Violence

"To hear her speak now, you would believe that I was a completely crazy, psychopathic monster who beat her up every day just for fun and every night was out screwing another woman while she was left stranded at home, starving with the children.

"That is the picture she paints but for about thirteen years she brutalised my brain and scandalised my name in her efforts to seize control of my mind. She had the general attitude that if she couldn't have it she would destroy it - and told me so.

All the while, she was always saying how much she loved me. No, it wasn't just jealousy, there was something else, something was seriously wrong.

Physical Violence

"I remember one time, very early in our relationship, when she was first pregnant, she started hitting me because I didn't come home the night before and my attitude was wrong. I did not want to fight with her but she wouldn't let me escape, get out of the house, so I tied her up, left her on the bed and went out until she cooled down. Obviously her punches could not do much damage to me but she had a habit of hitting, scratching and verbally abusing me when ever she was angry.

"A few years ago when she slapped me on the side of my head, I realised, thinking back, that she had hit me about twice as many times as I hit her. I remember one time I had scratches and cuts all over my face, arms and body which took several weeks to heal. Another time she sent a lunatic friend of hers to attack me with a knife and afterwards said she was 'sorry' he didn't kill me, the father of her three children.

"Her physical assaults had - relatively - very little effect on me but the non-physical attacks, with her sharp wit and acid tongue, hurt very, very deeply, especially in the presence of our children or other people. Sometimes I would be traumatised by the shit she was spewing up. Sometimes I feared that if I didn't do something to shut her up, people would think, especially the girls, that all the nastiness she was saying about me was true. Sometimes I would lose my temper and hit her and every time she would appear to be the victim and I the criminal.

No Excuse

"The use of violence - of any kind, physical or non-physical, regardless who is dishing it out - is not a human right.

Sometimes it may appear to be the only means left to safeguard our human rights but it is not itself a right. So, if I appear to give reasons as excuses for why I violated her, it is not to justify my own violent actions, but to give a clearer understanding of the environment in which I operated.

"I admit that I had said and done things to her which I can't be proud of and for which I have apologised to her and our children many times and tried to make amends. But I think what hurt her most was what I did for myself which she saw as against her. I do admit that I hit her several times over the years, and I believe that if it was only once, that would have been once too often. I even went to her house one time with a knife with the clear intention of killing her - but fortunately, didn't. If not for the presence of our daughters, I would now be in prison and they would be motherless.

Non-Physical Violence

Power Play

"I moved in with her a few months before our first child was born. There were a few hiccups but we managed to focus our attentions more on the child. One particularly cold winters night when I came home later than she desired, she told me to get out of her apartment. I said 'OK' and left. At that time I had nowhere else to go so I slept in the car until I found alternative accommodation at my parents' place.

"When I went back for my belongings a few days later, she had changed her mind. She told me, instead of walking out as I did, I should have said I did not want to go and she would have let me stay. In other words she wanted to see me squirm and hear me beg for the privilege of staying in her house a little bit longer. I left anyway.

"Over the next ten or twelve years ***she*** terminated our relationship at least ten times. Each and every time, after a few days, weeks or even months, she would change her mind and come looking for me.

"Why did I take her back after the first time? After the umpteenth time, I asked myself the same question. Some say it's love, but there is no sensible answer for such foolish behaviour. I can think of three possible reasons for my actions:

1) I needed the challenge of learning more about myself under pressure

2) I thought we could work things out if <u>she</u> changed, if she stopped lying and gave up her quest to control me because <u>I</u> was not about to change, I wanted to retain control of myself

3) sex. I just loved having sex with her - don't ask me why, maybe it was an addiction. You know how difficult it is for an alcoholic to turn down her or his favourite drink. Most of the time, sex with her was magic.

Communication

"I think communication played a major role in our relationship. We talked a lot about all sorts of things. We even communicated mentally over distances. But I think the most important aspects of our communication were the lies. She is a damn-blasted liar. In all the time that I have known her up to today I have never lied to her once. Not even once. But she started lying from the beginning; from her first response to my declarations about the kind of person I am, to one of the very last direct questions I asked her.

The Lies

"Most of her lies were to do with her extra-relational sexual activities. She knew that as far as I was concerned, she was free to do as she pleased and she didn't need to lie about it. But she could not allow me that kind of freedom because the idea of me screwing around caused her too much stress so she just did her thing and lied about it (unlike me who told her the truth as it was).

"For example she got me to unwittingly finance a weekend romp with one of her lovers by telling me she and the girls were going to spend time with relatives. I found out that a famous Rasta dub poet who I was producing at the time was performing for two days at a festival in the same area. I called both days and found that my children were with their relatives but their mother wasn't.

"Over the next six months she repeatedly denied screwing anybody. She told me it was my dirty, sick mind that would think such a filthy, unprincipled thing about her. Wasn't he my professional colleague and she my faithful woman? She explained that both times when I called she was out shopping. But nothing she said supported the facts. Nothing added up. As the months dragged by I became more and more confused and disorientated. I started to doubt my own sanity as she insisted I was in need of professional psychiatric help. In her own words I needed to have my head 'seen to'. I did agree to go and get counselling a few times but only as a couple. Each time she refused - point blank.

"She couldn't understand why I was so happy when I found them together and she finally admitted the truth, that I was right all along. But how could she understand my joy? Insane people cannot understand the value of sanity. I was so happy to know that I was not crazy after all; that it was her and not my mind that was playing tricks on me. Of course, she explained that they had never been together before that weekend or since - but then later on she accused me of destroying their dream relationship with my insane jealousy.

"Imagine her fury when he confirmed that I had told him long before that weekend that he could have her if she wanted because she was not my property.

"Another time, after I discovered what she thought was a secret abortion, she explained that it was because I gave her a sexually transmitted disease (STD) - which I didn't have any sign of - and the *doctor* advised her to kill the child because it might be deformed. The truth is, she could not be sure who the father was so she decided to remove the complication with the help of a girl 'friend'. She killed what was probably my child without any kind of consultation or any indication that it existed and then blamed me for the act. She still doesn't know the real reason why her friend was so enthusiastic about 'helping' her out.

"Towards the very end, when we were having some problems, I started getting some strange vibes from my children as well, I became suspicious, so I asked her whether she had a lover. After some hesitant, diversionary tactic she admitted it.

"I asked: 'Do I know him?'

'No.' she answered.

"It turned out that this was a fellow student of hers, a guy whom I had met through her a year before, and had seen him many times since; I had even left them together at her place on at least one occasion late at night, expecting and believing that was what she wanted, even though she had told me that there was 'absolutely nothing' going on between them. Would you believe that this man whom she referred to as a 'stupid little boy', an 'idiot' and a 'half-wit' in casual conversation, had been living with her for about three weeks and she had told my daughters not to tell me about it?. Can you imagine their state of confusion?

Pain of Silence

"Other deep and lasting impressions she made on my spirit include lying to our daughters, telling them repeatedly that their father is not well, he is crazy. I must admit though, that many of my angry reactions to her stimuli - my own lunatic behaviour - tended to reinforce the portrait she was painting of me. Most of the time I found myself unable to contradict the lie - even when I wanted to - because that would have meant putting a blight on her image instead of mine. Either way, it's the girls who would lose out in the end. Sometimes, I felt even my dumbfounded silence was confirmation, like the time she told them in my presence that when they get to be seventeen and they have to see a psychiatrist, it will be because of a 'genetic inheritance' from their father, me, because I'm sick. How do you defend against that kind of attack? Is it a healthy person who would tell their children that, simply to hurt the other parent? It wouldn't matter to them which of their parents was sick if they were going to inherit it anyway.

Identity

"When she called me a 'Black bastard' earlier in the relationship, it was such a shock, I eagerly accepted her 'slip of the tongue' explanation; I even created some of my own excuses for her. As time went on and I experienced some of her derogatory comments about her darker 'friends', I realised that she, just like most 'mixed-race' Africans, has a very serious, possibly fatal, identity problem. This is not to say that "unmixed" Africans are not just as mixed-up with other identity problems. With her Ancestors, she hates Europeans ('I hate them, hate them, hate them!'), fears, envies and despises Africans, can't trust Arabs and has no knowledge of or regard for Malaysians.

Deepest Cut

"Of all the things this woman did to me, I think the one which hurt me the most, which made the deepest hole in my heart, was when she said that it was my fault that our fourth daughter died. A huge chunk of my best feelings for her fell into the abyss. Our precious little girl was born premature, like two of her other sisters, with all kinds of complications to her respiratory and digestive systems. She had two major operations before she died in our arms, nine days old. We were devastated by her death. I actually believed, until her very last breath, that she would pull through; she put up such a heroic struggle.

"I don't think this woman actually believes that our daughter's death was my fault; she said it on more than one occasion but how did she arrive at that conclusion?

Gratitude

"Throughout our relationship I tried to help her to develop her talents, fulfil her own potential and become independent of me and everyone else but instead of saying 'thank you', she always used the facts to curse me. For example: she was an art-school dropout with a little talent but even less opportunity. I started a greetings card business to publish her drawings. She was unable to pursue it. I asked her to produce the sleeve for my second album - twelve years and 4 LPs later, it has not been done.

"Along the way, I realised she was a brilliant and creative cook. I spent 2 years setting her up in her own catering business which she is still operating today. After many years of profitable trading, she said I forced her into the catering business because I didn't want her to succeed as an artist. At various times she would tell me and everyone else who would listen, that she had to survive with the children on her own because I was never around to help.

Love

"Contrast that with a statement which she made round about 'half-time' in our relationship. She said I tricked her into believing that I loved her when in fact I didn't care a toss about her. I asked her how many times had I told her that I loved her. She said 'Never'. I asked where did she get the idea from that I loved her. She seemed very upset and confused by the question and its possible implications but she answered that it was the way I acted; it was my dishonest behaviour that fooled her. She said that since I didn't love her I should have told her so and let her get on with her life instead of *pretending* that I did.

"I asked her: 'Which would you prefer, someone who treated you as you would like to be treated, as you would expect a person who loved you and cared about you to treat you? or someone who treated you as his worst enemy, robbed you, undermined you and brutalised you but told you every day how much he loved you?'

Future Prospects

"Yes, I learned a lot from this relationship. If nothing else it has taught me the value of believing in my own judgement. I have always been able to 'suss' people out but I didn't always follow my initial instinct. I can't blame her for what she did or what she is, I have to take responsibility, at least, for being in the ring with her - she didn't tie me down. She is who she is and what she is and had no choice in the matter but I could have reacted differently or left her alone.

"It may appear as if I have changed because it is now less likely for me to be violent (physically or otherwise) in a personal relationship, but I don't think that my character has changed, I am still very independent, short-tempered and militant. What has happened is that I have learned how to avoid people and situations in my private life which tend to test my patience to the limit. Now I have much fewer personal, sexual involvements with women because I pay more attention to the fine print, the little indications of their inner character which may be in contention with mine.

"I also found out in this relationship, how destructive a lie can be and how important a lie is to the liar - in some cases, more important than life itself.

"Towards the end, when she realised that there was nothing else that she could do to touch me, that I was really gone this time, she chose to use the girls more blatantly and decisively, as her secret weapon. She tried police and court injunctions but they didn't work, so finally, she tried alienation. Not surprisingly, after lying to them all their lives about what was happening between us, she has been very effective with the two eldest girls, who have now chosen not to communicate with me.

"Even less surprising is her relative lack of success with the youngest one, who still continues to see me. This is my daughter whose early, awkward to answer questions exposed a precocious logic and an independent spirit that has managed - so far - to withstand the combined onslaught of her sisters, her mother, her grandmother (who has always hated me with a passion) and her mother's 'friends', in favour of knowing her father. And I am thankful to the Ancestors for that. I hope the Ancestors bring us together to share some of this precious life while we still have it."

Amy

Amy is an employed secretarial administrator who admitted her own use of violence in her involvement with an alcohol-dependent man who dictated what she could wear and who she could see but says that her violence was always in retaliation to her partner's attacks. She also made some useful suggestions of questions which can be asked in a future, larger research project.

Nature of Violence

"Violence is being subjected to something that you shouldn't have to be and it is totally unnecessary.

Communication

"There wasn't really any difficulty in communication, we used to talk about lots of things but just when he'd had a drink he was unreasonable, he might say something to me that I didn't agree with and I would try to put my point across but he wouldn't listen. He didn't want to listen because he had a drink. There wasn't any specific area where there was lack of communication because when he hadn't had a drink we communicated on everything.

"He wouldn't talk about it afterwards. I mean he'd never say 'sorry' after he'd hit me or anything. He would just carry on as if nothing had happened and if I brought it up then I was exaggerating and it used to end up in an argument so in the end I just didn't bother. So I suppose lack of communication on both our parts was a problem, yes. He wasn't prepared to communicate all the time and I just got fed up with trying to.

Cause of Violence

"As far as I know it was just the drink which caused the violence, whether he had some sort of mental block on me that only came out when he had a drink, you know, if he didn't like the way I was in certain areas and that, but it only ever came out when he had a drink. That's the reason his first marriage broke up because he was horrible after he'd had a drink. He always admitted to me that it was his fault his first marriage broke up and he knew it was the drink but no, he didn't think he had a drink problem. He's just one of those people that go out and have a drink and think he's fine. You can't <u>make</u> someone decide that they have a problem, it's something they have to decide for themselves. I don't know why he carried on.

"I really don't know why I stayed in it. As I said it was only the drink that was a problem, apart from that, we had a very good relationship. So I suppose I just sat there thinking 'perhaps he won't drink as much'. The good times were good, so I suppose they sort of made up for the bad times. Plus, I was brought up in a relationship that was very violent; my father was violent towards my mother, so ... I mean, you know it's wrong, that it shouldn't happen but because you had been brought up that way, you tend to think 'well it does happen' and people put up with it. That's one of the reasons why I kept trying again.

"It just got to the stage where he was getting more violent, I mean each attack was worse than the previous one and I was also pregnant. If I wasn't pregnant I would have probably stayed; the way I looked at it, if it was just me that was at risk ... but I didn't want to risk the life of my unborn child.

"His attitude was that if you're with someone, you put up with them - no matter what - and he should be entitled to have a drink if he wanted a drink. It had a lot to do with the way he was brought up; he was Irish catholic and basically old fashioned in that the man is the boss of the house and he can do what he wants and the woman is there to look after him and put up with everything.

"I don't agree with that at all. I'm not the subservient woman and that's probably why we had such a violent relationship because I wouldn't let him walk over me.

Future Prospects

"I know what I want from a relationship and what I am not prepared to put up with but whether you get it or not ... I mean you could be with someone and they can be wonderful for about six months and then you both get complacent and you change and things aren't as easy going. I'll probably make mistakes again.

"I think it should be down to parents to tell their children that they should treat others the way they would like to be treated themselves. It's nice to be nice. That's the way I was brought up. If parents took more interest in the way their children are towards other people, then I don't think you would have as much violence."

Mary

Mary is a professional woman who worked for some time in a women's refuge in Australia where she grew up. She said that she had not experienced physical violence but volunteered to be interviewed because she felt that she could contribute some valuable information about some of the battered refugees she and her colleagues tried to help. Before the recorded interview, we spent a whole hour just chatting about the project and some of the difficulties I was experiencing. As we relaxed, the interview became more of a discussion with Mary fielding as many questions as I did; some of my answers and comments are included in this section (all in italics) because they help to clarify some points which are made elsewhere in this book. We found as we talked, that some of her own experiences were just as harrowing as those of some of the women who went to the refuge.

Male Violence

"I think that because a man is normally physically stronger he is capable of committing violence against a woman. He is more able to control the situation by becoming violent."

I would say that in any relationship where there are problems there is violence. In the vast majority of relationships where there are problems the violence is not manifested physically, it's manifest in very devious forms in ways that people use to undermine each other's power. When you get to the point of being frustrated or angry enough you recognise that a little non-physical violence could settle the argument. When there's this violence going on it escalates to the point where each party would use whatever instrument is most appropriate at the time to achieve the objective of chopping up, cutting down, undermining, getting one over. And that's what most violence is about to settle the argument in your favour; the final arbiter.

"What's your argument where the parties are equally matched? like the situation which I was in where I was so frustrated, [*a different story from the one we will be discussing*] I'd say that we were in an equal situation because we were both frustrated and we were both mentally matched. There was no way this person could overpower me mentally - he was bigger than me so we weren't physically matched - but I also had a very sharp tongue, so together we were combatants of very equal stature and there was never - I don't feel that either of us ever actually 'won'. So how does that fit into your scheme [*that violence is the final arbiter*]?"

Yes it does because if you don't settle it that way in reasoned argument, it goes on the shelf till the next time. Where you recognise that you are equally matched you both convince yourselves at the time that you have given your opponent a good beating, so you both exit from the confrontation licking your wounds and each celebrating victory. There is no logic in the use of violence. You don't actually say 'If I abuse her or if I knife him it means my point is right' it is used as a rescue operation, a means of upgrading your position in your mind relative to the other person.

Trapped

"This is a situation I was in many years ago and the person was quite a number of years older than myself and I suppose in a strange kind of way I did get my own back eventually. When he would yell at me and be horrible to me I would shut down. Eventually what I did was I started having a relationship with somebody else that he didn't know about. That was a person who was very nice to me. That went on for some time and that's how I coped with his behaviour towards me. It was more like walking out the back door rather than running out the front door. My motives were actually to enable myself to easily leave this person. I was in a situation which I didn't feel I could just walk away from and I didn't feel I had the power to retaliate. The only power that I would have would be just the power to leave - eventually."

(*Why did Mary see having an affair with someone who treated her well, nicely, as getting her own back? See analysis of interviews*)

"I honestly don't remember any instances where I physically or mentally did anything to hurt this person. If you spoke to him perhaps he would say different, I doubt it though because I believe he would not even remember me. That would be his response. I mean this guy was the biggest bastard that ever walked this earth!

"That particular relationship is one where I felt that I was a victim of abuse because I didn't feel as if I was provoking or even retaliating. My reaction was actually to close down.

Just sulk, is the best way of putting it, that was it, that was my reaction because I felt that I couldn't retaliate.

"It's something that happened a long time ago but it's my memory of it and I still carry that anger because I didn't respond. I'm angry because I didn't. Well I'm not that angry really 'cause I did get out of the situation without hurting him. I didn't *give* him what he deserved but - now if I saw him, I would probably take a knife to him. Thirteen years later, I feel I could do that.

Nature of Violence

Rape

"I think the absolute worst kind of abuse is physical abuse, second to that is emotional abuse which can be as damaging, I agree, but I think that physical abuse is emotional abuse as well.

"No, he didn't hit me. He raped me. He didn't hit me".

In answer to the question "Has your partner ever done anything (apart from hitting you) which you felt was designed to or intended to cause you injury, pain, discomfort or disadvantage?" (see questionnaire, q.7), Mary said 'No'

"That's interesting. I wonder why I did that?

"I might have been confusing two different relationships but the answer to that question should be 'yes' not 'no'. It took at least three or four years before I could talk about that to anybody. Well I didn't think I had such a big problem with it anymore, I obviously still do have a problem with it. But like I said I'd like to cause that man some physical damage.

"I decided that my response of shutting down was my form of violence. That's when he would get really angry. For example, I would arrive at his house in a state of trepidation about what frame of mind he would be in. When he was cold I would just shut down because I didn't know how to deal with it, that's when he would get abusive towards me. Whether or not I need to take responsibility for that, I'm not sure. As far as I'm concerned I still don't think that I was necessarily responsible for this. The way I saw things he should have been saying to me 'look I've had a shitty day at work blah, blah ... that's why I am pissed off.' That's what I thought should have gone on. That situation would never happen to me now."

Cause of Violence

"What caused the violence between myself and this person? Well, I just think he was sick. And because I was young and naive I think I was tolerant of it. I think the person had very serious problems."

What would you do if your present boyfriend acted that exact same way?

"I would ask him what the problem was."

If you deal with the situation that way and it actually helps you to avoid a conflict and you can recognise that your dealing with it in that manner gets a different result, would you not say that you are responsible for the result that you get today?

"Yes"

Responsibility and Power

Well, if you are responsible for a positive result today, based on you reacting differently, how can you then be not responsible in the past because you got a negative result?

" I don't think that situation arose the first time, it came about. This situation came about after me saying to him 'have you got a problem?' and him saying 'no I haven't'. I mean this guy, he had many problems and I think that I would have got to the point where I made a decision not to ask him any more because I wouldn't get anything from him."

*If you say that what happens to you in a relationship is entirely dependent on what the other person does or how the other person is, you are renouncing all your power in the relationship. So when you say '**he** should have done this or **he** should have said that or **he** was such and such' you are ascribing to him alone the power to determine the outcome of the relationship. You have the power to determine the relationship, if you don't recognise and use that power consciously, positively, the relationship will be determined negatively against your interest with the aid of your unconscious, negative input. And since responsibility is a consequence of power, you are effectively relinquishing responsibility for your welfare, your future, your own life which you have invested in the relationship.*

*I'm not saying that you are responsible for him raping you **he's** responsible for him raping you and the consequence of that action. But, you are equally responsible for what happens between you and he. So if he rapes you, hits you or violates you in any way, you are equally responsible for the fact of the act because there are a billion things that each of you could have done which may not have resulted in violence against you. For example, you could have maybe, found a way to encourage him to talk or you could have, if you wanted to, seen that there was something wrong with him at the time and walked out. The responsibility is yours to make the next part of the relationship happen with your conscious involvement.*

"Yes, I see your point. Yes, yes"

However it 'came about', whenever it 'came about', from the very first moment you and he made conscious contact with each other, from that first moment every single thing that happened in the relationship you were both equally and totally responsible for - the good and the bad.

"Yes."

It's a very difficult concept to comprehend and accept when you're looking at a bad relationship but easier to accept with a good relationship.

"It's also easier to comprehend if you're looking at a situation from the outside. If I was in a situation like that at the moment, I couldn't cope with what you are saying at all.

Frustration

"I believe that men don't actually want to hit women. I sincerely believe that. I think that what happens is the conditions of just being male become so difficult that the frustrations drive that person to the point where ...

"There's a classic thing that happened with one woman who used to come to the refuge. Her partner, who I am sure really loved her and really cared about her, had a very high-powered job which put a lot of pressure on him. They had a super-expensive house, in the suburbs somewhere and he was basically not capable emotionally of keeping up appearances. She was one of these people who constantly wanted more; was gratified by having a bigger, better house all the time, she was putting pressure on him. He became violent to her because he couldn't handle the situation.

"I've got to the point where I've been so frustrated by a situation that I've wanted to commit physical violence against another person, but I haven' t done it. I mean I knew that had I done it the consequences would have been that I would have been hit back and this person was much bigger than me and much more capable of doing me damage than I was of doing them. And that was just because of a frustrating situation that we were both in and we couldn't see a way out. So I understand that it happens.

"After working in a refuge for four years I feel that women can't stop it on their own so we have to sort of get in touch with men and try to work out where they are coming from in order to combat it."

Communication

"I think communication was the stem, the root of all the problems. In retrospect, I don't think we communicated successfully at all. Initially when we were getting to know each other I think we did for the first month that we were together. But that's something that tends to happen anyway because you're interested in what's happening with your potential partner. I think that communication broke down very quickly once he felt that I was dependent on him emotionally. I think that's when communication started to break down."

Mary told of a situation where she went to dinner at her best friend's. "We have been friends for fifteen years and gone through the most amazing situations together; we've faced death together more than once we've travelled together, we've shared partners we've done all sorts of things. There's a friendship there that's based on stuff that I would never walk away from.

"Her partner cooked chicken curry. They know I'm a vegetarian so they took the chicken out of the curry. I was furious, I was absolutely furious. She could not see that she had done anything wrong. I felt powerless, I was so furious because I couldn't say anything. I didn't say a thing."

That is a good example. You see, you have a responsibility to yourself to educate your friends about your needs and the stupidity of their actions. If they did it out of ignorance and they cared, you would get the appropriate response and you would all benefit from it.

"I take your point, but I felt so powerless when it actually happened; I felt hurt, when I left there I was very, very annoyed but she had no idea I was angry. Three days later when she called me, I spoke to her about it, I felt empowered and she did apologise."

Prevention

This comment is not meant to be a contradiction to what you quite rightly, say about the need to leave a violent relationship. That has always been seen and is now generally accepted as the most progressive advice you can give to a woman 'just leave the bastard' and in some cases, 'take the children and go'. I want to go to a point before you have to escape from violence; I want to look at the prevention of rather than the escape from violence. What I would suggest is that people look more not at what happened to them but at what happens by them, from them, with them. I don't accept that because we are in a patriarchal society a woman is powerless and therefore violated - I don't accept that. The first step towards preventing violence of any kind in any relationship is to accept that you are going into a relationship as a person who has absolute power, not as a defenceless, powerless person whose fate is in the hands of your so-called partner; and the other person is also entering as a person who has exactly the same power. Each has the power - over themselves not over each other - to make and execute decisions about her or his life on their own behalf and to determine what happens in the relationship. When you both recognise that each of you has equal value[47] in this new entity, the relationship, which you have just created there is no room for violence - of any kind.

The second step is to be honest with your prospective partner and be honest with yourself because sooner or later the truth will flow and the real you will come to the fore, then it's downhill all the way for the relationship.

---

[47] R,S., *The Human Value,* Sukisa Publications, 1987. The concept of human value, the idea that all particles of an entity are of equal value within that entity, hence all human beings, though unique individuals with unequal properties, are never-the-less of equal value.

"I think you're right but I don't think that that is what we get in our society because it is a patriarchy. I mean, I do agree with you, I think you're absolutely right and I actually try very hard to conduct relationships with people along those lines. I still get very frustrated from time to time because I do feel powerless in situations that I'm in basically because I'm not getting what I want and it's about me not getting what I want when I'm asking for it. It's not really about power but I feel powerless, if you understand what I'm saying."

But it is about power. If you're not getting what you want out of a relationship that you chose to be in, at the point where you cease to get what you want out of that relationship you chose to be in -

"I can leave"

You can choose not to be in it. Rather than have yourself dictating to or terrorising or violating the other person because you are not getting what you want, you remove yourself from this thing which is no longer of value to you.

Future Prospects

"That situation took place a long time ago. The relationship lasted I think between nine months and a year and I learned a lot from it. I will never get into another situation like that. It was a very strong learning relationship. There's probably a lot of negative stuff that I do now because of that because there is still that stuff that I carry around with me.

"I don't think we are ever in a situation where we have enough information about what's happening in relationships; I think that there is far too much that we are given about what we should do and how we should behave in relation to other people. I'm actually starting to read a lot more about learning to like myself, learning to respond to my intuitive self - I think I used to do that but I lost that somehow somewhere along the line. I personally believe that that's the kind of information that we need. Western society is so fast and we grow up so quickly and we are given so much; we are bombarded with images of how life should be, I don't feel that as adults we are ever in a position to relate to other people successfully because we don't relate to ourselves sufficiently.

"Yes, that's exactly what I'm saying, we are bombarded with the wrong kind of information in particular advertisements on TV, magazines, that kind of information is what we are fed and it's really not healthy information about how to relate to people. But I think I am getting better.

"I think more information should be available particularly to women about how to get away from violent men and the fact that they don't have to put up with men who are being physically aggressive or emotionally violent. I think people have to be made aware, people have to know, that emotional abuse exists, and then know that 'you don't have to put up with it, you don't have to tolerate it, you can leave it'.

"I think the obligation society has as far as information goes, is to say to people 'you can leave, it's OK to leave' but it fails dismally. Instead it tells people, particularly women 'if you leave a relationship, no matter how bad it is, **you** have failed', that's the message you get.

"Society should also be giving people information on ways of living on their own. You don't *have* to be in a relationship, it's OK to live on your own. You don't have to be in a relationship. They are messages that we should be giving the children.

"I think it is rather idealistic to believe that harmony remains constant."

I don't believe that. What I said was that if two people go into a relationship accepting that each is in supreme command of self, they will achieve a harmonic relationship. It is idealistic but without ideals there can be no objectives. The ideal situation is to educate children from before they are born with the idea that outside of them there is no greater power; that there's no one outside of them who can or should make any decision that would affect them that they should not be involved in. That is completely, totally opposite, contrary to what people are actually taught daily in everything.

"I couldn't agree with you more. I couldn't express what you've just said more succinctly or better myself. I holistically agree with you."

Once you recognise that your power over self is threatened as I attempt to undermine your power in the relationship, you will do one of two things: either get involved in that war in which case we both lose or get out of my way, ditch the relationship. Either way I end up the loser.

"You are talking in ideals, I know, but I think you can work towards those ideals, one problem I have with what you're saying is apart from the pressures from my family, I felt an emotional tie to him that it was very difficult for me to walk away from."

The reason why you had that problem is not because of something lacking in you, it's not you that has failed, it's the way we are taught to attach ourselves to something or someone. It's an education, an environment, a totality.

"It's not just to do with relationship violence it's to do with environmental violence. We're killing this planet."

Chapter Three

Findings

Interview Analysis

Introduction

It is expected that every reader would have analysed each of these case stories yourselves. If it appears that the analyses are a little sketchy, it is because I have taken different aspects of each case as it is presented in order to build a clear overall picture of the findings not a detailed analysis of everything presented in each story.

I have tried as much as possible to avoid duplication and repetition without leaving out the essential commonalities, similarities and differences between the various cases.

Fiona

Fiona insists that she did not do anything to harm her lover but because of "the strangeness of his behaviour and his various instabilities", he *thought* she had. Her attitude to his culture and his background as "*strange ideas* about things" could not have made him feel very comfortable or unharmed, especially as she admitted to "cross-cultural misunderstandings".

She gives him the credit for *dictating* the terms of the relationship and "apart from cultural differences", for being the cause of violence. Here she does not recognise him as being a responsible person capable of making serious decisions, but sees him merely as a negative behaviour-pattern created by early child abuse.

Fiona insinuates that psychiatric help for *him* and enhanced communication could have resolved their relationship problems. She would have been very happy if he could have been adjusted to fit her.

She could help herself and future relationships if she can recognise and accept her own interactive part in the relationship, even where her own decisions and actions do not achieve all she wished or expected they would.

Abeo

is one of the few people who admitted that they were violent in the relationship but she went completely the other way (as a lot of people in her situation do), crediting herself with being the only partner who used violence. She is also caught up in the Euro-centric idea that good and bad and everything in between cannot exist in the same entity. She feels that if things are not working out and she is bad, he must be good; so she has to make excuses for or deny altogether his violence. His habitual use of stimulated sexual denial as a weapon against her was not seen as violence, even though it was clear to her that his intention was to cause her pain.

Christine

Her sudden realisation of the pervasiveness of violence in relationships was too much even for her to accept. She was able to understand that it was *they* who had a problem and not just him but it seems, from her story, as though he felt that *she* had a problem and not them or him. A very common response in problem relationships which usually includes ascribing the cause of the problems to the other persons past or some other intangible, unchangeable characteristic.

Patrick

Patrick says he was "never really violent" as he disclosed how he used non-physical violence against nearly all the people around him. He admits he was being "very psychological about hurting". He may have realised that he could get away with the use of non-physical violence more readily than physical violence because he could severely hurt people without them being able to show what he did to them, but if they retaliated physically he was in a position to have them reprimanded by other entities for attacking him.

He was also afraid of getting hurt himself. Which suggests that he would have become very skilful at using non-physical violence up to but not beyond the threshold of his victim's anger, where physical violence against him would most likely be his reward. This and his statement that he *decided* to "finish" the argument with physical violence, is in keeping with the idea that physical violence is usually reserved as the last word in the argument if the non-physical attack is unavailable or ineffective.

Like most of the other people interviewed, Patrick ascribes both his and his partner's behaviour to childhood experiences as if those experiences alone (and not the totality of all that they were, coupled with the particular way they interacted) were the causes of them violating each other.

For Patrick, counselling, as we spoke, was far from satisfactory because of lack of information from his unnamed present counsellor, unlike his previous counsellor Luke Daniels, who he felt was more productive because there was communication, a two-way flow of information. He was just left to stumble his way blindly around a maze of memories, fears, emotions, dreams, desires and imaginings. He was feeling trapped in a situation which is supposed to be ultimately a liberating experience.

One of Patrick's last comments "I may have *decided* to be violent instead.", gives a clue for the answer to the question of whether those who use physical or non-physical violence have a choice. The answer is "yes!" we all have an infinite number of choices how we act or react to stimulus.

Femi

Femi's story, spanning the longest period of time, inspires some very interesting questions, some of which he obviously attempted to answer himself. The most obvious question, which, ironically, is usually asked of women who complain of years of brutality in their relationships, which is: why did he remain in it for so long? he had difficulty answering. It is understandable that, as with most couples, something dramatic or traumatic happens, they split up; then something else happens and they try again to see if they can work things out a second time. But "at least ***ten times***"?

Two or three breaks in a relationship calls "time out" for both parties to look closely at themselves, at each other and at the relationship to assess carefully and honestly as Abi Ajoni advises, the pros and cons, the whys and wherefores of their union. Time to look see if it is at all possible to find a minimum common area in which they could relate harmoniously without recourse to physical or non-physical violence. If they could not reach such an agreement, time to accept their incompatibility as a fact of life and move on.

As there were children involved, it would have been necessary for them to negotiate a means by which the children could have the benefit of access to both parents and their relative families. This can be done with either no contact or minimum contact between the parents according to their mutual requirement. Difficult as it may seem, if they both saw the children as independent entities and respected the rights of each other as self-determinate beings, they would have found ways to relate, not necessarily as lovers, but harmonically never the less, without the need to subvert any of their individual characteristics.

Femi volunteered three possible reasons why he agreed to resume the relationship so many times. The first one is probably true of most of us whenever we do something risky or dangerously foolish. The third reason is true of any addiction where the addictive substance (sex) is freely available (maybe even enticingly offered), in close proximity with the addict and the addicted person has not undergone any successful detoxification programme. The second reason, however, is very significant. He thought they could work things out "*if* ***she*** *changed*"

Why should she change? If she believed that he was the problem, why should she change? But even if she did not believe he was the problem, why should she change? Why should she change herself to accommodate him or his preferences? She was not created specifically for him, like a tailor made suit which needs to be adjusted to fit perfectly. If he found her lying and her megalomania unpalatable but other aspects of her desirable, it was not for him to rearrange her to his liking. All he had to do was accept her as she was - totally - and work with the parts which are useful, or reject her - again totally - and move on.

The same things would apply to her.

But then again, maybe he did accept her as she was; maybe that is why he took her back so many times, because he wanted the good things more than he did not want the bad things. Maybe he was just *hoping* that she would change the bad things without him actually doing anything to her to affect the changes. I say that because I was in the very same situation and each time I took her back because I accepted her the way she was, the sweetness with the sour, but in the back of my mind I wanted to believe that she would change. What woke me up was the realisation that she was deliberately putting my life at risk, trying to kill me, and I could not afford that.

It is hard to believe that anybody can complain about being treated as if they are loved, but if what Femi says is true, if he is, as he claims, not a liar, it is in keeping with the rest of the story. Maybe all she wanted was to hear him say the words; after all those years of feeling loved but never actually hearing it. Her way was not to ask him but to batter him into confirming or denying it. He did neither. Either way she would have been satisfied because confirmation would prove her control over him and denial would justify her aggressiveness.

Femi's experience with his children being used as weapons against him is unfortunately, an all too common occurrence in the war of the sexes. Particularly in the African community, where a tradition of the extended families of both parents caring for the children have up to now been a major factor in preventing tragedies, increasing numbers of children are now growing up not having any contact with or knowledge of a complete set of grandparents, cousins, aunts, uncles, and other relatives and friends of one of their parents, usually the father, when the relationship dies. In many cases the denied parent is deeply hurt, but the real casualty is always the children, in more ways than we can imagine.

The practice of depriving children of their relatives or poisoning their minds against one or other of their parents need to stop now before we get to the point where it is common for blood brothers and sisters who have no knowledge of their connection to be falling into bed with each other or blood brothers and sisters to kill each other because they are from different parts of town.

Amy

At the best of times communication was good but when things went wrong communication broke down. Or was it because communication broke down things went wrong? Amy's partner had a problem with alcohol, it is true but she seems hell bent on using alcohol consumption as an excuse for this man's violent behaviour. I would agree with that to some degree if it happened once, where he had a drink for the first time, did not know what to expect from the effects of alcohol and boom! violence. But if that was not the case and the bottle did not hold him down and pour its whisky down his throat, there is no reason to mention alcohol as a cause of violence. It may be a tool or weapon used in the process of committing violent acts but it is not a cause.

It is just another way of trying to deny him responsibility for his own actions, including the use of alcohol when he knows the effect it has on him. His refusal to do something about it means that he is happy to play the role of a victim of alcohol. The whole beauty of it is that he could choose when and where to act irresponsibly and people would accept it because it's the drink not him, so he doesn't have to be responsible and grown up all the time. As Del Martin puts it: "violent actions often seem to be more acceptable - or at least more comprehensible - in our society when they are performed by a person who is intoxicated".[48]

Mary

In describing one of her relationships as "...combatants of very equal stature", Mary shows that she was so frustrated in that situation because even though he was physically more capable of doing her damage than she was him they always ended up at stale mate having used only non-physical violence in the battle. They refrained from physical violence because

---

[48] Martin,D., *Battered Women*, p.57.

he would have been afraid of the consequence to him if she was visibly damaged and she was afraid to initiate or wander into the domain of physical violence because of the possible consequence of physical damage to her which, in her own words, she feared more than the non-physical.

Mary's declaration that she had not experienced violence even though she had undergone one of the worst forms of violence one can experience, being raped by her partner, suggests that either her conception of violence does not include rape or as so many people who suffer from that type of violence, she ***blamed*** herself for it happening to her and therefore desired to suppress the fact of its occurrence. Here she would be confusing her responsibility for being party to the rape with blame for being the cause of the rape. She chose to rewrite her history without what she considered to be a blemish against her.

Rape is multiple violations. The rape itself is violence but other forms of violence both physical and non-physical are frequently used to terrify or subdue the victim sufficiently in order for the rape to be carried out.

In Mary's case her own diagnosis that her partner was "sick" compounded her fear of him because as far as she was concerned a sick person could and would do anything - if she upset him. Him being sick in her eyes does not exempt him from being responsible for his actions. Equally, her being "young and naive" does not exempt her either from being responsible for her actions, for being "tolerant" of his behaviour or just "shutting down". She was able and willing to acknowledge responsibility for a good relationship but found difficulty in accepting responsibility for the bad one, until she is shown that it is her own interactive input which determines the outcome of the relationship. One reason for that inconsistency, which happens with most people, could be her association or substitution of the word 'responsibility' with the words 'blame' or 'credit'.

Why did Mary believe that having an affair with someone who treated her well while she was being brutalised by her partner, was getting her own back on him? If she is his property, then offering herself to another person to use or enjoy without his permission or knowledge can be a serious violation of his rights. In fact if she does anything without his permission or knowledge, she is violating his rights.

Mary may be saying, with her statement that she considered her partner at the time to have some right of ownership of her. She may be intimating that she had promised him or agreed never to have sex with anyone else while she was with him. Many people make such agreements, for example with the marriage vows or lovers' bonding vows, and when, almost inevitably, they falter, instead of accepting that as human beings they cannot be certain of what they will or will not do and admitting the betrayal of their own promise, they lie. Not only do they lie, they also commit other acts of violence to cover up the original facts and the lies. For Mary to have kept the affair a secret from her partner as long as she did I expect she would have had to lie many times.

If Mary is not his property and she happens to enjoy the company and attentions of another person, if she is an independent entity who has a right to associate and interact with any other independent entity in any way they both choose to accept as reasonable and mutually profitable, her affair should not be of any concern to him.

If all she is doing is just being herself, whoever she is, finding other people who may be able to add positively to her experience of life, she could not be doing anything against him. He may well be upset by her finding comfort, or whatever she gets, with someone else but him being upset with who or what she is should not be her concern. If she cares about him but her way of being tends to hurt him without her intending to, then she could explain to him that what she is doing is not something *against* him but *for* her. If he still can't accept her the way she is, with all her needs and desires which he cannot fulfil; if he cannot allow her the right to do for herself what is good for her, then he should find someone who is more suited to his needs instead.

If she believes that what she is doing is correct and is essentially for her benefit and not against him, there would be no need to lie in order to cover it up. He will have to either accept it or reject it. If he didn't know that she was having an affair, as in this case, it is mere fantasy to imagine that anything was being done *to* him - unless his property was giving itself away.

Whatever the reasons, the fact that she saw doing something that was good for her as something against him is an indication that she did not see herself as a person who had a right to do for self, to satisfy her own needs, to fulfil her own aspirations and to determine her own destiny.

The Information Needs

The second stage of data analysis, which looked at all the data collected from both the field and desk research including the questionnaires, revealed an overwhelmingly strong feeling that there was not enough useful information available to couples before, during or after being in a relationship.

Most respondents felt that people should be instructed from school onwards on how to manage in a relationship; how to recognise violence in its more subtle forms; how to prevent it; what to do if it occurs; how to get help from other entities;

how to be caring partners, parents and friends. This was borne out by the professionals who said that their clients often came to them uninformed and confused about what had been happening in their lives. Those who recognised the need to educate people in general about the nature, causes and prevention of violence also associated education with schools but that is not where our education begins, it starts in the home. So basically we need to start re-educating the parents who are willing to be re-educated in order that they are able to educate their children by practical example, in the way they interact with each other.

There was almost unanimous agreement that public and private sector workers who are likely to have any kind of contact with people experiencing difficulty in relationships, should be better trained and informed on how to communicate effectively with people who may need their assistance.

The nature of the information given exclusively to African women and whether their information needs are different from those of Asian women or any other non-African women, convicted men, the general public, etc., could not be established because of the uncooperative and unprofessional attitudes of the African, Asian and 'multiethnic' "professionals" in the women's organisations which were contacted.

A Refuge Experience

Information supplied by Mary about her stint as a refuge worker gives some insight into the kind of information given to women who went to her refuge. She said:

"What we tended to do, the policy of the women's refuge where I worked was that women were responsible for their own lives. It's their responsibility to do what they liked. They came to us for safety. That was the only reason they came to us. If they asked us for information we would then provide it but our purpose was to be a place where they could go to get away from the violence. We would never encourage any woman to leave a relationship and we would never encourage them to stay in a relationship, but if they asked us of ways of leaving, if they asked us of ways of staying, we would do our utmost to provide that information.

"Most of the information we tended to provide was to women who felt they wanted to leave a violent relationship because most of the time it was violence. A lot of the time it was to do with becoming economically independent. Something you said before triggered off something that relates to the kind of information that we provided and that was that we believed we were a band aid; you could keep running from refuge to refuge to refuge, if that man wanted to find you, he would find you. We had women that went from state to state, Australia is a huge place but if they wanted to go to another place we would make sure there was somewhere they could go. That was the kind of information we would provide on that level.

"There was information available on emotional violence as well as the physical - just. Things like, men would threaten to keep the kids: 'if you leave I'll make sure you never see the kids again cause I've got the house. The house is in my name.' And women would believe that because they would be so frightened of never seeing their children again. We would try and encourage them to become more empowered, to believe more in their own [power] - we would try and repair their self esteem; to help them to believe that they were OK."

As has already been stated, it was not possible to obtain the legal professional's view of the information needs of their clients or the information which is communicated exclusively between them. *(see Methods*)

The Nature of Violence

What is violence? How does it manifest itself in relationships? As is clear from the statistical data of victims/violators (volunteers), not everyone is aware of the complex nature of violence or how it manifests itself both physically and non-physically in interpersonal relationships. Many people did not even answer the question as to how they would define violence.

The short definition I have chosen to use in this book is:

violence is any act which violates

this includes: every form of **physical** assault and the various forms of **non-physical** assault such as verbal abuse, repression, infringement or denial of rights, psychological, sexual, political, cultural, social and spiritual subversion, oppression and alienation of a person or persons. The definition of the word violence is itself a problem.

The narrow confines of physical force within which academics, sociologists, researchers etymologists and other commentators squeeze violence, does not bear with the "domestic violence" industry's recognition and use of a host of non-physical terms such as verbal abuse, emotional abuse and non-verbal aggression. Though the practitioners in the field even go as far as admitting that the non-physical aspects of violence is at least as destructive as physical force, they almost unanimously subscribe in practice, to the definition of violence as the use of physical force. If the Latin root of the word violence, *vis*, means power, force and strength, it should be clear to those who wish to see, that violence is the use of power, force or strength to achieve advantage over (empower); to disadvantage or damage (depower) others.

Those who should know better and in many cases <u>do</u> know better, insist on giving the impression that violence is only a physical thing and, more recently, only if it's an unlawful physical thing is it violence. The only reason I can see for that is **they do not want people to associate violence with the exercise of authority.**

That is why they refuse to accept that there is such a thing as non-physical violence. If non-physical violence was accepted as a concept, those in authority in society, who violate us on every level every day, would have to criminalise or illegitimise non-physical violence. They would then have to define non-physical violence. In so doing they would be describing exactly what they do to us, because that is how they manage to gain power and maintain control.

They would not want to define violence as I have done, but since they would have to include the non-physical in the definition of violence, they would simply qualify it with the word 'unlawful'. The dictionaries would say:

> violence is any **unlawful** act, whether covert or overt, which is intended to, designed to or calculated to cause pain, injury, discomfort, disadvantage to or otherwise harm or destroy, transgress or infringe on a person or persons;

That may sound like an oversimplified solution to a very complex problem but who would believe that a group of people (state controllers) who make the greatest use of violence (military, police, prison, mental institutions, schools, secret service, etc.) against a significantly larger group (general population), can criminalise violence and escape being treated as criminals, merely because they defined violence as the 'illegal' or 'unlawful' use of physical force.

The same way they have managed to legitimise the production of alcohol for the benefit of a few and made it illegal for the rest to produce, so they have managed to legitimise the use of violence for the benefit of a few and made it illegal for the rest to use it.

As more and more of us come to understand the true nature of violence, the state controllers are moving more towards the criminalisation of the non-physical aspects as well as the physical because they recognise that we are sophisticated enough to use it and prepared to use it to our advantage. In the mean time they are happy to use or support the use of violence in all its forms against the people under the guise of legitimate authority.

Many people voluntarily told me that they did not return the questionnaire because, even though it was supposed to be anonymous, they felt rather stupid when, having filled in half of it, they realised that their view of violence as just physical assault was all "wrong". What was wrong about their view of violence? Most of us experience violence on a daily basis but because violence in a violent society is so common place, it seems natural to be violated on some levels. Because we accept some level of violence as normal, we no longer recognise certain aspects of it as being violence.

The volunteers in interview confirmed lack of knowledge on the nature of violence; a common statement being "I didn't know that was violence". One person, who claimed to be non-violent (until a recent physical attack on his partner), admitted to using psychological terror all of his life on big brothers, parents, school mates, women - people who always appeared to be stronger than he in some way. He said it was a defence strategy which he suspected is used by women against men in situations where they felt disadvantaged by the men's greater physical strength.

It is clear, from the evidence of the interviewees that there was violence in all their relationships even the ones who did not recognise it. This tends to confirm the hypothesis that in any relationship where there are problems there is violence.

It may not be manifested physically but it is there all the same. It may be anything from "little" (or big) white(?) lies, psychologically undermining remarks and comments, to emotional terrorism and sexual coercion or extortion, where one partner forces the other into sexual intercourse by non-physical means; or stimulated sexual denial where one partner does things which they know will stimulate and arouse the other sexually but finally refuses to satisfy the awakened desire. These are violent acts which we may not see as violent because we see them so often as everyday occurrences.

For example, if we turn on the TV one day - any day, any channel - and eliminate every lie, every act of deception, every undermining manoeuvre, every attempt at suppression or repression of another's personality, every theft, every slander, every fraud, every swindle, every extortion, every threat, every scandalisation, every stimulated sexual denial, every sexual coercion, every aggressive insult, every subtle insult, every defamation, every profanity directed at a believer, every put-down, every stitch-up, every word of verbal abuse, in fact if you edit out every non-physical violation that passes without comment or condemnation, the screen would remain blank for most of the day and night. And that is without even mentioning the physical violence; the shootings, stabbings, punches, bombings, drownings, chokings, lynchings, rapes, and running over with cars, trucks and tanks.

That is the kind of society we are living in. Television reflects some of the worst aspects of society but the media does not exist outside of society it is part of society. We live in a society that glorifies and rewards violence; the soldier who kills the most people becomes the hero; the business man or woman who swindles and steals most effectively acquires status and power; the politician who lies and cheats most convincingly becomes prime minister or president and the conniving lover who tells you what you want to believe gets your body. And sometimes your mind as well.

The professionals interviewed said that as counsellors they could not dictate to their clients a definition of violence, or even give a broad outline of what they believe violence to be, but in discussing their experiences the clients would sometimes come to recognise that something which they accepted as "normal" like pushing, shoving, shouting, undermining, lying, etc. were in fact violent acts and could lead to more extreme forms of physical violence. They both agreed that non-physical violence is more difficult to deal with because of its intangibility; "In a long-term sense, it's often the emotional violence that is the most insidious and the most destructive to the person",[49](*see also Akbar*[50]).

It is not just the intangibility of non-physical violence which makes it difficult to deal with but also its commonality. Because the everyday aspects are so commonplace, they are not seen as requiring exceptional attention; and also because they are liberally employed by most people who succeed in this environment, or by their agents.

Children, who are the most precious and sometimes most desired consequences of female/male relationships are also the most violated of all people. They are seen as prized possessions of their parents or the state or some other kind of designated institution. They are regularly denied their rights as independent, self-determinate beings, as adults arbitrarily

---

[49] Walton,J., Interview tape 1993

[50] Akbar,N., *Chains and Images of Psychological Slavery*, New Mind Productions 1990 p1-2. He states that: "The slavery that feeds on the psychology, invading the soul of man, destroying his loyalties to himself and establishing allegiance to forces which destroy him, is an even worse form of capture" than physical shackles. p2

raise and lower age limits dictating when children can be allowed to think for themselves. Those who take it upon themselves to exercise their human rights are brutally suppressed and their spirits broken. They are beaten, sometimes mercilessly, by their parents and other elders with the blessings of the Christian church because they say, God told them if they spare the rod they will spoil the child. They are terrorised into submission and moulded by their parents, not necessarily into what they would like themselves to be but into what the parents would like them to be. Again this is done with the sanction of the church because they say, God told them to do it.

It may well be because all his clients have previously been convicted of using physical violence that Daniels seemed more preoccupied with the physical aspects of violence. He was also very much aware of and concerned with the violence of both private and public institutions sanctioned by the state.

It was not possible to establish what information is communicated exclusively to and from women, in particular African women, by and to the professionals on the nature of violence, due to lack of co-operation on the part of the women's organisations contacted.

There is, generally, a consensus of opinion that a comprehensive analysis of violence, its nature and its causes, which will empower individuals with the means of prevention, is urgently needed.[51]

The Causes of Violence

On the question of causes of violence, 67% of the lay people interviewed said it was the other partner, the rest either did not know or gave some external intangible such as the system or patriarchy, one person said it was herself and

[51] Rodgerson,G. and Wilson,E., (eds.), 1991 p15

another said it was his past, being an abused child. It seems, from the evidence, that none of those factors on their own would cause violence, but all of them in their particular context of interaction - their relationship - resulted in violent interaction.

Many of those interviewed said lack of knowledge of their partner's background, their own history, lack of self-esteem, ignorance of the opposite gender and each other in general, lack of or misleading information in general on conducting harmonic relationships, lack of communication, inadequate or destructive communication, and the other person's unstable emotional or psychological condition were contributory factors in causing violence between them.

While the professionals recognised the capacity of both partners to be violent, they cited historical and external factors, such as the offenders themselves being hurt as children, the "socialisation of violence" in a racist, patriarchal society and the "sexism in a society which informs men that they are the bosses, that they should be in control over women's lives and that women are not as important as they are" as the main causes of violence.[52] It became obvious that the same type of information directed at women, that they are the powerless victims and men are the powerful aggressors[53] is also given to men. Never-the-less, the counsellors accepted that regardless of any historical, environmental, biological or other factors which make up the complete individual, it is not the ***condition*** of that person but the ***interaction*** between them and their environment (including their partner) which result in violence of any kind from either party. To say that one party's biological, environmental or historical condition is the cause of violence in any relationship is to attempt to negate the

---

[52] Daniels,L., Interview tape 1993

[53] See Literature Review

responsibility and power of the other parties in that relationship altogether.

Again, it was not possible to establish what information is communicated exclusively to and from women, by and to the professionals contacted on the causes of violence, due to lack of co-operation.

Nearly all violent partners suggest that the other party is not blameless, at least partly responsible. They confuse blame or credit with responsibility, as McBeth found when she visited men in prison. They complained that the women "provoked" them,[54] as Daniels confirms, "Sometimes they [the men] get angry and rage about what has *happened* to them".[55] It may well be time to take notice of what the convicted or otherwise recognised perpetrator of physical violence has to say about what they believe caused her or him to do what they had done, instead of just shutting the problem away in prisons[56] and/or allowing them to relinquish responsibility for their actions with excuses of biological or sociological programming.[57] [58]

Many of us believe that by blaming someone else - who we recognise must have something to do with the way we interact with them - for the result of our interaction, absolves us from taking responsibility for our own actions. However, in relationships, it is very often the case that someone who is totally blameless for a particular incident is never-the-less equally responsible with the other person who can be seen to be completely at fault for the incident. So often I have heard the statement from my own children who, just a minute before were playing happily with each other, "He (or she) did this (or that) to me".

---

[54] McBeth,F., 1992

[55] Daniels,L., Interview tape 1993

[56] McBeth,F., 1992

[57] Rodgerson,G. and Wilson,E., (eds.), 1991 p36

[58] Mama,A., 1989 p84

Inevitably, when I ask: "What caused them to do that?" the answer is: "I don't know".

Then, "What did you do? what happened just before he (or she) did that?" Nearly always the answer is: "Nothing". Even now, talking to adults, the result is the same; they start off by saying they did "Nothing" and then move on to: "no normal person would react the way she did, she's crazy" or "but that does not give him the right to hit me"

Of course nothing you do - even an act of physical or non-physical violence - nothing gives anyone the <u>right</u> to violate you in return. The fact still remains that you are ultimately responsible for everything you do - irrespective of why you do it. You may say "I did that because she did this" or "He did that because he's a man, so I <u>had</u> to do it, what else could I have done?" therefore, you say, you are not responsible for the action. But you are responsible. Not only are you responsible for your every action, you are also responsible for the consequence of what you do - good or bad - as you interact with your environment. And you are equally responsible with all who you interact for what happens between you.

Most people cited the cause of violence as something to do with their partners or ex-partners but as some eventually came to understand or admit, the cause of violence was also *something* to do with themselves. Ultimately the cause of violence in <u>any</u> relationship is the particular interaction between the parties of the relationship. Recognising that no person comes out of, or exists in, a vacuum, each party in a relationship is a complex entity which has characteristics forged by biological, cultural, emotional, environmental, historical, psychological, social and spiritual influences. As such, it is reasonable to expect that each person will bring with them all these influences which make up their complete selves, not just one cardboard cut-out characteristic such as child abuse.

It would be wrong not to take into consideration the enslavement of the African nation when considering the cause of violence in a relationship which includes one or more African people, but it would be equally wrong to suggest that the reason why there is violence in the relationship is because one or more of the parties are suffering the effects of slavery. In the first instance you are not considering the whole relationship nor the complete person because you are leaving out a significant portion of the person's most recent history and therefore a considerable amount of information about the relationship. In the second instance you are also not considering the complete person nor the whole relationship because, by focusing on only one aspect of one party's characteristics you are at the same time obscuring or rejecting the multitude of other characteristics which make up the person and denying the interactive input of the other party or parties in the relationship.

The difficulty most people have in accepting responsibility for any part of a bad relationship is based on the erroneous idea that it reduces the other party's culpability; that it reduces the victim's status as victim or nullifies the degree of victimisation. They are trapped in this Eurocentric "either/or" cultural dogma which does not recognise complex wholes only uni-dimensional parts; which does not accept that a person can be good and bad, criminal and victim, and everything in between, at the same time, in the same context.

That is why it is so difficult - impossible in most cases - for some people to accept that they themselves are equally responsible for what happens between them and their partners, or that a child is equally responsible (with all those who are supposed to share responsibility for it) for what happens to her or him.

To explain the concept of equal responsibility which carries with it the equally difficult idea of equal power in relationships, we would need to write a book of several volumes. Never the less, I will try to introduce the idea here:

Two adults who are each responsible for their individual actions and equally responsible for the results of a new entity they have created called a "relationship", conceive a child - a fourth entity - as a consequence (good) of sexual intercourse or some other kind of action. They are both responsible for the child, for what **they** do with the child, to the child, for the child, against the child or about the child. While the child is incapable of action, it is the parents' duty to fulfil their responsibility for the child which their actions caused to be created. Responsibility for the child does not mean ownership of, control of or authority over the child. Responsibility for the child is as one is responsible for the *consequence* of one's actions nothing more nor less. One's responsibility for the child remains for as long as the child exists - even into adulthood.

When the child is capable of any action - including thought - (and that stage can only be determined by the child), it is responsible for every action of hers or his. If it is hungry and it cries, it is responsible for that; if it is hungry and it does not cry, it is also responsible for not crying. So the child interacts with the people of its environment and how it interacts determines the outcome of the relationship with its environment, its mother or its father or its grand parents, etc. So the child is responsible. But the child's responsibility for itself and its own actions does not in any way negate nor diminish the parents' responsibility for the child.

If the child is in an environment or situation where it is at risk, this is as a result of its interaction with its parents, (or whoever is nominally charged with looking after it at the time), and interaction with its environment. If the result is positive the child is given credit such as how brave and independent or precocious he or she is, the parents are given accolades for producing such an outstanding person. This is the result of interaction with her or his environment for which the child is responsible and, if the child's actions were conscious, calculated and/or deliberately executed, rightfully, credited for.

When however, the result is negative, for example, the child gets assaulted, there is no recognition that the child has any input into the situation. All the responsibility for that particular outcome is given to the attacker or the society or the parents or the police or any number of other entities whose shared responsibility for her or his safety and well-being can not be in doubt. The child's responsibility for what happened is denied by all even though this negative outcome, just like the positive consequence, was also the result of the child's interaction with its environment.

Being unaware of what we are doing does not diminish our responsibility for our actions, nor does lack of awareness of the possible consequences absolve us from suffering or enjoying the consequence. Ignorance or knowledge can help to reduce or increase the degree to which we are blamed or credited for the act and its consequence but they can have no bearing what so ever on the question of our responsibility for ourselves, for our actions and for the consequences of those actions.

Prevention of violence

On the issue of prevention there was unanimous agreement from all the interviewees, lay and professional alike, that more and better communication between the couples could help. People need to be encouraged and taught how to communicate productively with each other.

Most people felt that lack of information of the correct type was a major factor in the amount and type of violence they had in their relationships. Therefore more relevant information of the type which gives the recipient a feeling of self-worth and gives them an understanding of their true value and power as complete, self-determinate human beings is necessary. People need to learn how to take responsibility for their lives and be able to allow others the same privilege.

There was also unanimous agreement that more social provision could be made by government for supporting victims and dealing with perpetrators of violence in the short term and educating everyone generally, including school children, about violence in both the short term and the long term. Raising the level of awareness generally, including pre-involvement counselling for couples on the nature and causes of violence was seen as a good preventative measure.

Femi's situation reminds me of a song I wrote called '*Be Love*'[59] which was inspired by the lies and dishonesty of my partner at the time. She never expressed any appreciation of the song, either musically or lyrically; she didn't actually say it was "crap" as she christened "*The Human Value*"[60] but predictably, she gave the general impression that it was less than credible. Part of the song said:

If you really want to show me you love me
Be Love to me
You never have to tell me you love me
If your love is real
Just Be Love as love is...

---

[59] R.,S., Be Love, *Third World War (LP)*, Zara Music Records, Sukisa Publications 1983

[60] R.,S., *The Human Value*, Sukisa Publications, 1987. The concept of human value, the idea that all particles of an entity are of equal value within that entity, hence all human beings, though unique individuals with unequal properties, are never-the-less of equal value.

You batter me with lies
And then you stab me
With your daggers of 'truth'
And when I start to cry
You say you love me
Deep down in the root

But action is stronger
And just a little gesture
Means more than a thousand
'I love you's
So Be Love as love is ...

Many people believe that words are not important but then expect the magic words "I love you" to heal all the wounds of a barrage of abuse, emotional assault and psychological terror. It works for a while with some of us but eventually, common sense intervenes.

No matter how loving or caring a person is to you, if that person imprisons you, does not allow you to be who and what you are, how and why you want to be, you will eventually violate that person in return or co-operate with your own violation. The most effective way to prevent violence is through self-determination, an unflinching, uncompromising, universal self-determination which recognises and respects all people's rights to be free. Once you have tasted freedom, even in your dreams, and recognised its value, you will see no need, nor desire to violate anyone else. That is why I say "freedom first and then peace will last"[61]

Due to lack of co-operation, it was not possible to establish what information is communicated to and from women by the professionals contacted, on the prevention of violence.

---

[61] R.,S., *Freedom First*, title track of L.P. on Zara Music Records, Sukisa Publications, 1984

The African Family and State Violence

Too often we hear it stated that the reason why the African man is violent to himself, his woman and his children, why the African woman is abusive to herself, her man and her children and why the children are self-destructive and homicidal to each other is because of the effects of slavery, the legacy of colonialism, capitalism, racism or some other kind of European "ism".

All of these reasons, so expertly presented by many of our great and not so great social and political commentators, why we are generally self-destructive and terrorise each other are very accurate, perfectly true and undeniably real. Within the Global African community there is a tendency to ascribe to external forces the blame for the "disintegration" of the African family and the responsibility to rebuild it. But it is also true and undeniably real that we have been active participants in our history and as such we are equally responsible as anyone else, (though not at all to *blame*), for the state we are in, regardless what they have done and are still doing to us.

It is a fact that we are existing today and have been for a very long time, in a state of war. We are in a state of war and every single African person is a war survivor. We owe our survival to the valiant struggles of our Ancestors both on and off the continent as they interacted with Arab invaders in the East for more than a thousand years before the European invaders from the West with whom we have been struggling more than five hundred years now.

Instead of blaming ourselves, the Europeans or the Arabs for the dismal state of our family relations, I would rather **credit** ourselves for being here, still, after so many hundreds of years of genocidal attacks (following thousands of years of invasions) some of which were even conspiratorially co-ordinated as our enemies advanced on our continent from the East and West, North and South.[62] We are responsible for the fact that we are still here, that we are still struggling and that we will go on struggling until we are free, in possession of our lands, our bodies and our minds and in control of our destiny.

It is indeed arguable whether we would be so self destructive if we were left to our own devises, to interact with each other as we please; it is also a fact that if we did not have some input into what happens to us, we would not be here today as a global nation - scattered and disorganised but here, nevertheless - and none of us would be relating to each other at all, much less as harmonically and productively as some of us do.

Some of us recognise that we have a responsibility to ourselves; history teaches us that our actions as individuals, positive or negative, has an effect on our lives, positive and negative. Today, all around the world we are under attack. We are under attack as individuals, as a family and as a global nation. In order for us to deal effectively with these attacks we must understand their nature, how they are launched and how they are intended to affect us. We must create combat strategies to deal with the problem as a global nation, as families and as individuals.

If the level of physical violence in a society and the use of it by that society is to be the standard for measuring how civilised (or otherwise) the people are, then, a closer look at the violence of the European nation - Global Europe - and their relationship with the rest of the world over their relatively short period of global interaction, should reveal the most savage, barbaric, uncivilised, immoral, amoral group of people in the history of human existence. We would find that

---

[62] **Williams**,C., *The Destruction of Black Civilization: Great Issues of Race from 4500 B.C. to 2000 A.D.*, (2nd edition) Chicago: Third World Press 1988.

historically, Europeans have been responsible for the destruction of more human beings than any other nation of people since time began.

In this context, we find ourselves survivors of a continuing war, trying to circumvent, change or eliminate some of the laws, traditions and practices which tend to undermine our community. Laws such as the Children's Act in England, which, although it is supposed to place the child's best interest as its primary concern, does not take into consideration the special circumstances of a child's cultural environment, when considering how that child's care should be handled in relation to its parents, relatives and other interested parties. So, you find a judge making decisions about an African child, using a check list designed to be relevant only to a European child.

Unemployment in the African community is three times that of the European community and the African man is more likely to be unemployed than any other person in British society.

Social Security legislation tends to affect more seriously the African family than any other. This is especially true with the so-called "single parent" African family, where traditionally, the woman is living alone with the children and the man is living elsewhere. He could spend even more time with the children than say, a European father who is actually living in the same house but spends most of his time at the job, at the club or at the pub. Yet the system is heavily weighted against the African man and his family.

The unmarried mother has up to now, before the parental responsibility provision of the Children's Act (England), had full authority in relation to custody of the child or children. This state of affairs was the basis of many a sour relationship turning even more rancid because of the woman's destructive exercise of her legal rights and the man's frustration at having no legal rights as far as access and custody of the children were concerned.

The only legal avenue open to the father in a situation where the mother was not at all willing to give the child access to its father and was legally able to abscond with the child without any notice to the father, was for the father to make the child a ward of court. A decision which I felt I had to take after one of my children was taken away from me and flown out of the country. I don't believe that it is right for any African person to put their child into the hands of the European state, but, as a last resort, I did it.

I did that because I feel that **it is a child's indisputable, undeniable and irrevocable human right to have access to both her or his parents**, (even if that right of access has to be enforced by the state), until the point where the child decides that he or she does not want such contact with either parent. And the child's decision should also be respected and protected by everyone, even by the state. Any person who prevents any child from having access to her or his parent(s) is violating the child. Where the desire or need for contact is mutual, then the rights of the parent is also being violated.

The consequence of such violence, where, as in some recent "ritual abuse" cases, the state takes a child from its parents and prevents contact or makes no provision for safe contact between them, is even more deadly violence. Such children, because of the way they had been socialised (or not) may seek personal partners or circumstances which are more likely to give them the opportunity to combat as an adult the pain of childhood by reliving the violence of involuntary separation. They may find great difficulty forming relationships where violence, in all its guises, is not a primary ingredient.

In a society which sees African people as second class citizens and in many cases not even citizens at all but all too visible aliens, the relationship between us and the police who are usually on the front line of the attack against us, is generally a confrontational one. This unhealthy relationship is made even worse when the police are called to intervene in a domestic dispute. There they are likely to use violence above and beyond their ambiguous legal remit against one or both parties to the dispute.[63]

The violence continues to escalate as the courts are filled with half-truths, lies and statistics. Tougher laws and more prisons are called for to contain an increasingly criminalised African population. As the family becomes more and more fragmented all that is left for us as children are memories of things which we can not understand but know very well are not good for us.

As young adults we see the circle of violence broadening to include everything we would like to accomplish being denied us while the same circle of violence engulfs us, contracting, squeezing, squeezing our hearts out, till all that is left is an empty shell, reaching outwards, grasping for anything, anything because we believe we have nothing; dying for anything because we think we have nothing to live for.

We **fall** for the promises and lies of crooked politicians and equally crooked middle men and women who say they represent Allah, Buddha, God, Krishna, Marx or some other kind of saviour because we are not strong enough, able enough or informed enough to **stand** for ourselves.

I beg the Ancestors that we, Global Africa, will not let ourselves fall for the next massive con trick that Global Europe is already playing on us because that promises to be the worst, most destructive genocidal attack any people have ever made against any other people. I am talking about the issue of population control.

---

[63] Campbell,A. and Gibbs,J.J., Eds., *Violent Transactions*, Basil Blackwell, 1986

The recent Population Control conference[64] which promised the "empowerment of women" as their campaign motto is nothing less than an attempt to legitimise a Global Europe mass genocide conspiracy against the Global African nation and other non-European nations with the aid of a few elite, ignorant and/or traitorous Africans, Arabs and Asians. Europe is six times more densely populated than Africa according to the United Nation's own distorted demographic figures.[65] Yet these thieves, liars, puppets, stooges and their criminal partners would have you believe that Africa is overpopulated. Over the past three hundred or so years while the Global African population was being decimated by war, enslavement, mass poisonings and strategic viral infections while other nations increased their populations fourfold, Global Europe's population increased an astonishing ***sevenfold.***[66]

The population control pundits say, very straight-faced, that less people equals more development. You don't have to be a doctor of demography or development expert to know that is a lie. They suggest that if African women, some of the most oppressed and impoverished people in the world, have only one or two children, they would become less impoverished, less oppressed and more powerful because they would have less child-rearing, more free time to study and develop themselves. Thcy and their children would therefore become more productive, more advanced, both individually and as a nation. Another big lie. History has taught us that greater population means greater potential for development and expansion and less people means less power. After all it is the people of any nation which is its greatest asset.[67]

---

[64] UN conference on Population and Development held in Cairo, Egypt, 5-13th Sept. 1994

[65] Aset, "DIY Genocide", ***Global Africa Pocket News***, Vol.1, #5, and "Population Control is Genocide", and others ***GAP News*** Vol. 1,#7, 1994

[66] Information Project for Africa, *Excessive Force: power, politics & population control*, 1995

[67] Information Project for Africa, *Excessive Force: power, politics & population control*, 1995

One of the effects these lies tend to have is to confuse and disorientate the people, who instinctively know that they are lies but want desperately to believe their "leaders" and academics who are supposed to know better. Another effect is to cause even greater friction between African men and African women. Most men, who still see the wisdom in having large families, especially in rural agrarian societies where most African people live, are being accused of exploiting African women by using their bodies purely as machines for producing babies. Some of us see it as an absolute necessity to produce as many African people as possible to compensate for the mass destruction of our youths, the siphoning off of our nation's lifeblood.

Some African women, who are expectedly, tired of being oppressed by everybody, especially their own men, may be willing to see some value in the twisted illogic of the European's "small family is better" propaganda argument. But one question they need to answer is: if there are too many people in the world and small families are better, why are Global Europe paying European women to have multiple-child births and rewarding successful experiments that produce European children beyond the menopause? (see **GAP News** for more information).

Population control is not a new concept. Europeans have been trying to reduce the African population ever since they found that there were more of us than them.[68] What is new, creatively simple and devastatingly destructive, is the means by which it can be achieved quickly, effectively, with the greatest support and active involvement of the victims by co-opting their leaders and policy makers while ensuring through media propaganda and other manipulations, that the people do not know or suspect what is happening to them.

---

[68] Cress-Welsing, F., Colour Confrontation & Racism (White Supremacy), C-R Publishers 1970

If the Global African nation is willing to believe that Europeans or any of those criminal/confused Africans and others who are now peddling the population control and development con are doing it for our benefit or for some kind of humanitarian good after our long and painful lessons of experience at their hands, we deserve to be totally erased from the face of the Earth with no record left, not even a word, that we ever existed. If we are able to learn from our experiences, the next century will see the development of an African family ready to take its place at the head of the human family. We will surely triumph.

The Non-Violent Option

I was recently chatting with some self-confessed anarchist people who insisted, very adamantly, that they were pacifist. Of course, I had heard some time ago that there was such a thing as a pacifist anarchist but I had never had the pleasure of actually meeting one, much less three at the same time in my own car. I wondered aloud how a person attempting to be self-determinate in an oppressive and violent environment, can avoid using violence. They said, that they refrained from violence because violence breeds only more violence. But they took that statement a little bit too far when they said: therefore non-violence, or passive resistance is the only way to win your freedom in this violent society. I said that non-violence breeds even more violence. They pointed out that no violent revolution has ever achieved any freedom for the people who chose to use violence to overthrow the government of the time. Again, they too were only talking about physical violence, focusing on the military aspects of revolution.

I asked them whether there has ever been any successful revolution achieved through non-violent means or whether it is possible to have a peaceful revolution at all.

One of them gave Gandhi and his peoples' struggle for liberation as a good example of passive resistance working for the benefit of the people. Another person gave Martin Luther King Junior and the non-violent civil rights movement in the USA as a more relevant example.

I said that Gandhi was a perfect example of pacifism working against the interest of the oppressed.

One of Gandhi's greatest qualities and also one of his greatest lessons to us all was his courage and his conviction to do what he believed was right and stick with it to the very end - even if he was wrong. And how wrong can you be?

Mahatma Gandhi went on hunger strike twice, determined to fast to his death, at a time when it appeared that his people were on the verge of taking control of their country by force. He may have realised that power was about to be snatched from the hands of the Europeans and their local representatives in the ruling castes, of which he was a member. The people loved him (or more accurately, what he promised) so much that both times they stopped killing, stopped fighting altogether and waited for him and his associates to resume and complete "negotiations" with the British government.

They stopped moving towards their own liberation because a man who was in the process of committing the greatest act of violence that any human being can commit, was telling them that he was against violence. Gandhi and later Martin Luther King Junior are held up to the world by those who live by violence and profit from violence, as the greatest of leaders because of their commitment to non-violence.

There were many levels at which the Europeans and their lackeys were violating the rights of the people of India. When

I think of what Gandhi did, the great effect he had on world history, I see many, many questions; I begin to wonder what concept he had of the nature of violence or what he thought he was doing.

Did he, the guru of modern day non-violent activism, see violence merely as the *unlawful* use of *physical* force to cause damage to person and property? Or did he believe that it was violence to cause someone not to be educated; to cause someone to be homeless; to cause someone to die of starvation; to so demoralise a person that the spirit dies; to so terrorise a nation that the only way they can see out of their pain of living is self-destruction? Did he believe that the body which he was using was a sacred temple; that it was not anybody's right to destroy it?

If the killing of Gandhi by a gunman was violence, why is Gandhi's attempt to kill the same body by starvation not violence? Why is he being celebrated as the "father" of non-violence?

Maybe one of you suicidal pacifists out there could educate me on the difference between the two acts. Maybe you can show me why the deaths of Bobby Sands and scores of IRA hunger strikers was not violence. Maybe you can show me why the death of a young mother who overdoses on a cocktail of alcohol, crack and malnutrition in a Philadelphia slum is not violence. Maybe you can show me how an African man or woman "jumping" to their death out of a fifth floor window because immigration terrorists are looking to lock them up and then deport them is not violence. If you can show me how those clear acts of self-destruction, all motivated by violence, are not violent acts, you will begin to convince me that Mahatma Gandhi was a non-violent person.

Martin Luther King Jr. is a quite different kettle of fish. He also, was a man of tremendous, unflinching courage who gave his life for what he believed in, but some people believe he was a little more naive than Gandhi; since he was very familiar with the Gandhi experience, he should have known better. He allowed himself to be manipulated, used and abused by a small group of Europeans who, had firmly established themselves as the economic controllers of the African community. They saw the growth of a militant movement of African people as the most formidable threat to their socio-economic power base. They knew they could not stop the movement so, as they would a raging river, they decided to divert it.

Through their control of the media and other information institutions, they conspired to promote non-violence as the only way for African people to achieve our human rights, which they termed "civil rights". They felt that a passive, disoriented, consumer-based, self-destructive African community would be more profitable than a militant Africa-centered, freedom-fighting, self-determinate and productive African community.

This group, which of course, included Europeans of all religious and secular colours, were disproportionately over-represented by a group of Europeans who themselves had suffered hundreds of years of social and religious persecution. They felt that it was in their interests to promote non-violence to solve our socio-political and socio-economic problems while at the same time promoting internecine warfare and self destructive behaviour within the African community as a normal way of life.

These people, predominantly European adherents of the Jewish faith, were even more disproportionately represented in this conspiracy than they had been over-represented in the enslavement of African people.[69] These are facts which most European Jews go to great lengths to ensure that very few

---

[69] Historical Research Department of the Nation of Islam, *The Secret Relationship between Blacks and Jews, Vol. 1,* Latimer Associates, 1991

African people find out about. They will even attempt to suppress a whole book because of one sentence or paragraph such as this.

The problem with King is, he did not appear to know that he was being manipulated until, as his last celebrated speeches show, it was too late. He did not realise that he was encouraging, aiding and abetting the use of violence against himself and his own people when he advocated that they should just do nothing except march, sit, prayer and sing songs while a bunch of redneck state troopers and pigs with dogs beat their brains out.

Now, I hear you say: "What has all that got to do with non-violence in relationships with violence?". A lot. Everything. Freedom is the right of every entity to determine what happens to it.[70] If we are involved in a society where one group of people violates us individually and collectively, as a global nation, it is our duty and our right to do something about it; to ensure that their violation of our human rights cannot continue to be profitable to them in any way and to teach them that we will stop at nothing to guarantee our human rights.

If you are involved in a relationship where your partner violates you, it is also your right and your duty to yourself as a human being to do something about it. **So what do you do?** Anything you do which is intended to be directly or indirectly harmful or injurious to your partner is a violation of your partner. It is violence. The fact that your partner may be using violence against you does not mean that your own actions are not violent. If you do things or act in ways which are designed to undermine, upset or otherwise cause your partner a "problem", you are using violence; it may not be physical violence but it is violence, nevertheless.

---

[70] R.,S., *The Human Value*, Sukisa Publications, 1987.

Typical "pacifist" actions such as stopping of work and withdrawal of services or favours may well achieve the desired effect of reducing or transforming the opponent's violence but if such actions were designed to upset, undermine or negate your partner in any way, they cannot be non-violent acts. They may be merely retaliatory or reactionary but violent all the same. A person who professes to be non-violent or pacifist must **not** use violence in any form to achieve any end.

The only correct response of a *"true" pacifist*, if he or she chooses to remain in a violent relationship, is to *invite* the offender to discuss the situation and express her or his displeasure with the offence then *ask* the person to refrain from repeating the offence. If the violence continues, the pacifist partner has one of three avenues open to them:

a) continue to repeat the request

b) do nothing, accept it and pretend it's not happening or

c) get the hell out of there

Many of us know from bitter experience that merely *asking* someone who profits by the use of violence to stop violating does not work - even if they listen to you. Listening is not one of the bully's finer traits. So for most pacifists, history will just continue repeating itself if they choose to use route 'a'.

There is nothing a violator likes more than a compliant victim. The compliant victim in most cases saves the perpetrator the trouble of having to use physical violence to get or retain control. So we find the route 'b' pacifist hiding in a "non-violent" relationship where violence is endemic because they choose to accept the non-physical (sometimes even physical) brutality.

Route 'c' is the way most sensible people (pacifist or otherwise) would go once they find out that the particular person they were intending to relate to is not the right "mix" for them. This realisation and its related action can come at any time in a relationship from the very first moment of contact to many decades down the road.

One problem a "real" non-violent pacifist would have is whether they would employ the violence of a third party such as the state law enforcement machinery to deal with the persistent harassment (violence) of the ex-spouse who will not take "no" as a valid response. There are many people who say that they are non-violent but call the police or some other kind of thugs at the first opportunity, then pretend that they had nothing to do with the person being shot or beaten to death. A truly non-violent person can not and will not use violence under any circumstances, directly or by proxy, not even to defend herself, himself or their loved ones.

So, effectively, for a non-violent person (or group of people) there is no defence in this life against a violent person or group of people whose objective is to use or abuse the body or bodies of the non-violent person or group. A non-violent person (man or woman, boy or girl) can be raped or otherwise violated and cannot participate in or tacitly condone any violent act by any third party to punish the offender or prevent the offence from happening to her or him again.

So how does non-violence prevent violence? It does not. Non-violence cannot prevent violence. It is true that violence breeds violence but non-violence breeds even more violence. What prevents violence is the understanding by one entity that its use of violence, physical or non-physical, to exercise power over or gain control of another entity will <u>not</u> be tolerated and any and every means will be used to prevent it. Therefore violence for them can <u>not</u> be profitable.

Which reminds me of a similar argument during the period of the Global Europe "Cold war" conspiracy, East vs. West. Here were two global power blocks, supposedly mortal enemies, because of "diametrically opposed" political ideologies.

For more than forty years, many millions of Africans and a few more million non-Africans died fighting themselves and each other in numerous wars on one side or the other. Yet not a single East or West European died at the hands of an opposing European army in battle. Why? We are told that the reason why they didn't fight each other was because they both had the nuclear deterrent. And most of us believed it.

The truth (as time and history has proven), is that they are part of the same gang involved in a wicked global conspiracy.[71] The question I asked then and I ask it now is: ***if*** nuclear arms is such a great deterrent against war, (and there have been over one hundred wars around the world since 1945) why not let every country - *everybody* - have one? Better still, let each hold the trigger of the other's bomb. That could be one hell of a party.

The argument, from both sides, was that the other side was a bully and that the one side being the champion for righteousness and justice would use their nuke power if necessary, to protect the rest of us. The difference between their argument and my argument is that I am advocating the same rights for **all** people, to employ whatever means are necessary to achieve and maintain self-determination; they are advocating the right of Europeans only to manufacture, own or control any kind of arms including nuclear arms.

Which fits in very nicely with the idea being fed to the rest of the world that non-violence is the only way to progress, while they carry on using violence against the rest of us. Non-violence is no answer to violence. Non-violence in the face of persistent violence is the road to self-destruction. The non-violent option is <u>not</u> an option.

---

[71] R.,S., "Towards 2000", *JOMO:* Journal of the Pan-Africanist Congress Movement, May '91

The Healing Process

Every act of violence in a relationship, whether physical or non-physical, creates a wound in the violated. As time goes by, if these wounds are not helped to heal properly, they tend to have a fatal effect not only on the relationship but all too often on the individual parties to the relationship.

Every wound which is not treated promptly and carefully becomes a festering sore which, in time, occupies the most prominent position in the relationship. Before long these "sore spots" become so pervasive that there is hardly any subject, hardly any area of interaction the parties can touch without inflicting or experiencing pain.

In this society of the walking wounded, where violence is a normal daily experience, it will be difficult to find anyone whose psyche is not infested with open sores or unhealed wounds. The old saying that time heals all wounds is not quite true. Time alone does not heal untreated wounds. Just like their physical counterparts, emotional, psychological, social and spiritual wounds will, in time, develop protective scabs if they are left undisturbed for long enough. However, the longer they are left untreated, the thicker the scabs would become and the more difficult it would be to penetrate them in order to apply the necessary healing remedies.

Every time we enter a new relationship we carry previous, old wounds with us. The success or failure of our relationships depend on how we deal with or treat each other's wounds. Whether we add newer injuries to them, dig them and make them worse or try to help heal them, would tend to determine the depth, quality and length of our relationships.

But how do you treat a wound which you cannot see? The wounds of non-physical violence and of psychological or emotional trauma suffered as a result of physical violence can not be bandaged, stitched up, balmed or medicated in the same way as physical injuries which are visible and tangible. Nevertheless we need to apply the emotional bandages, we need to get out the psychological needles and do some nifty stitching; we need to apply the spiritual balms and we need to make positive use of reparative medication. We need to do all those things and more. There may even be times when we need to perform radical surgery such as the removal of self from the environment, the removal of items or the termination of practices which one or both of the parties may appear to be inextricably attached to but tend to have a negative effect on the relationship, in order to save the relationship and/or the lives of the participants.

The first and most important ingredient in the treatment of non-physical injuries is communication. There must be clear, accurate and honest communication of the damage experienced and the pain felt by the person or people who have been attacked or feel they have been attacked and the nature of the wound created. If you feel you have been wronged, you owe it to yourself to inform the other party of your injury in a way that he or she is more likely to understand and more enabled to appreciate your pain. It may even, in some instances, be necessary to demonstrate to the less sensitive how it feels to be treated in the manner you had been treated. Statements such as: "it happened such a long time ago", "forgive and forget" and "let bygones be bygones" are always welcomed by the violator but are never of any value to the violated or in resolving the problems.

By the same token, once you understand that your partner has been hurt by something you may or may not have done or said, you are in a position to try to help heal the wound. What is important at this stage is not whether you were the cause of the pain; the important factor is that your partner is in pain and you care. And because you care, your desire is to try to help ease the pain. It may be that the wound was not caused by your action, nevertheless, your care and attention, could still be of value in the healing process.

If however, the wound was caused by you but accidentally, you must demonstrate clearly that it was not intended, that you are truly sorry and are willing to do whatever you can to help repair the damage and help heal the wound.

If, on the other hand, the wound was wilfully inflicted either in retaliation for some damage you believe, rightly or wrongly, that your partner has done to you or as a means of establishing control and exercising power over your partner or even as a means of undermining and degrading her or him, the healing process becomes much more difficult to complete.

The slightest bruise to the spirit, the smallest bump on the emotion, the tiniest nick to the psyche, if ignored or aggravated, can have a serious, even terminal effect on the person and the relationship. The fact that the intent was to violate the other party, makes it difficult to demonstrate a desire to repair the resultant damage. But an understanding that the relationship will not harmonise, that it will not improve until the wounds have been healed, could in some cases help to motivate the desire to heal. Why? Because you care. If both parties care about each other and about the relationship, there is greater likelihood that they would desire healing.

Of course, many relationships with open, unhealed wounds often appear to be happy and carefree to the casual observer. But most such liaisons are doomed to end with bitterness and pent-up rage on one or both sides. The only way to ensure that people can relate harmoniously after painful experiences caused by violence is by going through the healing process.

The complete healing process would normally be in five stages, all of which would include a good dose of interactive communication. They are:

1) **damage assessment.** This would include communication of the fact that one party has been hurt (or at least *feels* hurt) and exploratory analysis through discussion to establish the extent of the damage, the cause and depth of the pain.

2) **guilt acknowledgement -** acceptance of responsibility by the violator for her or his actions and their consequences. This is of vital importance because the process cannot go any further without her or his desire to make amends. For example, after the recent genocidal civil war in Rwanda when many people were talking of reconciliation and forgiveness, one woman who had lost all her family said "Who can I forgive? Nobody has said they are sorry. How can I forgive?" Before you can ask for forgiveness you have to admit your guilt.

3) **expressions of regret**, remorse, compassion, etc. from the violator. You may admit your actions, you may even say "sorry" as the pope recently said on behalf of the Roman Catholic church for their part in the enslavement of African people, but unless you are prepared to *show* that you are genuinely repentant, such an admission may be no more than an idle, wicked boast and you will be unable to move to the next stage of the healing process.

4) **compensation** or **reparation** to the violated for the hurt they had suffered. This could include materials to be given or services to be rendered by the violator. It could also include symbolic, ritualistic and/or realistic retaliation by the victim in the form of structured, *mutually acceptable* physical and/or non-physical assaults; these symbolic or actual attacks would tend to remove the need in the wronged party for satisfaction and to reduce the desire for vengeance outside of a controlled environment, at the same time, they would also tend to give the wrongdoer a feeling of security in her or his own mind after having "paid" the penalty for their crime.

5) **reconciliation** (or **separation**). Only after the first four stages have been completed can there be real reconciliation. We can try to forgive and in many cases, readily forget but often, the desire for retribution, satisfaction and vengeance will at some time manifest itself in the form of some kind of violence. Reconciliation can take place when the violator is satisfied that the victim is satisfied and there is no fear of a surprise revenge attack and the violated is satisfied that the attacker is repentant. At this stage freer more open communication between the parties can result in a deeper understanding of themselves and each other which could bring them even closer than they had been before the violence.

There is also the possibility, after all has been said and done, that the two entities come to recognise that it is in the best interests of all concerned that they separate. Not as enemies, which would have been the case had they not gone through the healing process but as mutually respectful independent people who, because of their different or similar characteristics happen not to be suited for each other.

So, whether the result is reconciliation or separation, application of the healing process would guarantee a less violent, more harmonious relationship than would otherwise be possible, to the benefit of all concerned, especially the children.

The healing process could not work without the co-operation of both the victim and the perpetrator. Where, as in some very rare cases, only one party is violent, that person must acknowledge their action and agree freely to participate in the healing process. However, this kind of healing process is more likely to be tried and more likely to work in a relationship where both parties recognise that the violence is mutual (even if they manifest in different ways) and the harmonisation of their relationship is important to them both.[72]

---

[72] Spartacus R. is available for lectures, conferences and Healing workshops. For bookings please contact the publisher. (*See address and telephone number at front.*)

PART II

Chapter Four

Methodology

Generally, the methods used and the means by which information is obtained for books of this kind are not normally disclosed to the reader but left to the imagination of those who have a curiosity about what happens behind the scenes. With this project however, some of the difficulties experienced in trying to access necessary information were at least educational in relation to the subject matter. The methods used by others to sabotage, frustrate or prevent the research from being completed, were clear examples of violent, destructive and deviant behaviour. I have therefore decided to include a review of the process of information gathering for this project.

Data Collection and Analysis

As a way of achieving the overall aim of providing a deeper understanding of relationship violence, data was collected by means of both field research and desk research and the analysis of the data was conducted in two stages as follows:

Data Collection
Field Research, Desk Research,

Data Analysis
Preliminary Analysis, Final Analysis.

Data collection

The field research

consisted mainly of :

a) a questionnaire

b) interviews with victims and perpetrators of violence

c) interviews with professional practitioners and others involved in seeking solutions to and disseminating information on the problem of relationship violence

a) The Questionnaire

is one way of getting sensitive information from people who wish to remain anonymous and/or who ordinarily, would not be accessible. For the sake of convenience in terms of monitoring, accessibility and variety of racial, cultural, religious, national factors and to a lesser extent variety of ages, it was decided to use the students, lecturers and workers of the university as one of my target audiences.

The questionnaire was distributed on the university campus at Ladbroke House, Kentish Town, Spring House, Eden Vale and Holloway Road, by the self-selection method using a single location where it could be collected. A large number of copies of an A4 size leaflet (*Appendix B*) were posted up at all the above mentioned locations including Ladbroke House. This leaflet/poster gave the readers a brief outline of the research project and asked for people who had experienced any form of violence in a relationship to come forward and offer their assistance by filling out the questionnaire and possibly being interviewed as a follow-up. They were told where they could pick up or otherwise get a copy of the questionnaire and then given the option of returning it to the same location or if they prefer, to further guarantee greater anonymity, posting it directly to the address which was both on the front covering page of the questionnaire and the bottom of the leaflet/poster.

This method of distribution was chosen for several reasons:

1) it is relatively cheap (the cost of producing a questionnaire of 8 pages and a cover letter would have been prohibitive if distributed on a random blind basis).

2) a higher response rate was expected because it was felt that the questionnaires were more likely to be completed and returned if they were not being imposed on someone arbitrarily as say, by random post or by just being handed to them out of the blue in the street.

3) the single location pickup point was chosen because the sites are quite a distance apart and it would have been time-consuming, disruptive to other studies, expensive and energy-sapping to have had to run around from one site to the other first finding someone at each location who would be willing to take responsibility for keeping control of the questionnaire, then checking on them periodically to retrieve completed questionnaires or leave more.

4) collection would be easier and cheaper because respondents had a choice of depositing questionnaires with the administration office free of charge to themselves or returning them to the address given on the covering letter (there was however, one person who asked for a copy to be sent to them at one of the other sites).

The negative aspects of choosing this self-selection method are:

1) that some individuals could be excluded who might have filled out a questionnaire if they were handed one anonymously in an obviously random and general manner say, at a train station. But those same individuals would not expose themselves to scrutiny and possible, unwarranted, unfair judgement by directly asking someone for it. Similar to the kind of stigma that has been attached to purchasing contraceptives in the past. It would also be likely to exclude many people who had been the perpetrators of both physical and non-physical violence whose guilt would prevent them from coming forward.

2) there would be a narrower range of answers than with a truly random distribution because only people who had actually experienced what they considered to be violence, would ask for a questionnaire. There would therefore be less people saying in the questionnaires that they had no experience of violence, a statement which, as seen from the answers in a few of the questionnaires, generally meant no experience

of *physical violence* but usually masked the fact that there were other forms of violence being perpetrated (sometimes mutually) in the relationship (*see Cases and Analysis*)

3) the fact that some people become so traumatised by their experience of a violent relationship, especially one where the attacks were of a psychological or emotional nature, that they are incapable or unwilling to express any account of it (a feeling related by someone who, having requested that a questionnaire be sent to her, found it extremely painful and therefore impossible to complete the questionnaire), whereas if she was guided through the completion of the questionnaire she might have benefited from the experience

4) another negative aspect of this distribution method is that people had access to the publicity posters, (also a positive factor). Consequently, after just two days, a person or persons removed all the leaflets which were posted up at Ladbroke House, this meant that no one could find out about the project or the request for help. That did not stop the project. Another batch of leaflets were printed with a special message to the culprit(s)/vandal(s), (*see Appendix B*) and posted up the following week.

To this day, it is not known why the posters were removed because there was no response to the request that they should make direct contact if they had a problem with the writer or the contents of the poster. By way of speculating as to motives, questions were asked with the reply that "Two or three" women had asked for a questionnaire, assuming that the writer was a woman, but when they were corrected that the researcher was a man, an African man, they became angry and abusive to the receptionist and refused to take the questionnaire.

It is not known whether those women had anything to do with the removal of the questionnaires or whether the cartel of lecturers, both female and male, including Eileen O'Keefe, Nicholas Watts and the staff of the Child Abuse Studies Unit (CASU), who complained to the Dean and Head of School amongst others, about the research had any more to do with it. They spoke of many issues relating to the project including: "(a) legal; (b) ethical; (c) methodological; (d) the status of the project; (e) the quality of the supervision; (f) the lack of *consultation* with CASU". They were promised that the final marks will "reflect" their concerns.[73] None of them ever contacted me directly.

Someone, however, did remove the posters and it did cause serious problems with the research. It is also understood that a certain lecturer had been saying that the writer was dishonest in not declaring in the poster that he is a man. Why? Why should a person undertaking research on relationship violence declare their gender? Does the researcher's gender have any greater influence on the facts as they existed before the beginning of the research than the colour of her or his eyes or their shoe size? It is expected that every aspect of who the researcher is would have a bearing on what facts he or she has access to and makes use of and finally their *interpretation* and analysis of the facts. It would appear to me that if a person is interested in having the truth known about a subject which they have knowledge of, they would want to find ways of influencing the quality of the information which is

---

[73] Internal memoranda from and to the Dean of North London University, Jenny Somerville.

gathered. If they want accurate, honest information to be broadcast about the industry which they have a vested interest in why did none of them approach me at any time with information which they felt would improve the research? Why did they ignore my invitation?

Those are issues I would have liked to debate with the lecturer in question but the person who told me about her statement said she did not want to reveal her identity and refused to give reasons for her stupid comments. Such cowardly people who recognise that their positions are basically indefensible are usually smart enough not to try to defend them.

The bulk of the questionnaires were personally distributed in a controlled random manner, that is: every fifth person I met in my travels was handed one. This had the effect of reducing any bias of selection and extending the geographic range well beyond the boundaries of the University. Some people actually telephoned me to get questionnaires, having heard by word of mouth and the posters. Apart from the controlled random method, copies were also distributed by the self-selection method to people who approached personally and asked for one. They were given because it was felt that they wanted to help and they would therefore be more likely to respond than the majority of randomers (there is no way of checking this because there were no special marks applied to any of the questionnaires to identify their source in any way).

To broaden the scope of the research a few organisations which deal with relationship problems were targeted. They included Relate (London Marriage Guidance), Everyman Centre, Camden Black Sisters, Women Against Rape, Southall Black Sisters, Asian Women's Centre. Copies of the questionnaire were distributed to: Camden Black Sisters, the Everyman Centre and the Asian Women's Centre. Single copies were sent to each of the others as part of the introduction to the project.

Of all the completed questionnaires which were returned 36% of them (32% female and 4% male) indicated that they would not mind being interviewed. Edited transcripts of some of the interviews have been included in this book. It was not possible to make the necessary arrangements with all the potential interviewees for various reasons of conflicting schedules and time constraints. I had to complete the project on time for assessment.

b) Interviews with Volunteers.

Firstly, questions of clarification peculiar to the information contained in each questionnaire were asked, i.e. where there were inconsistencies or if the meaning of a comment was not clear. Then the same four questions were asked of each person (*see Case Stories and Appendix D*).

It is not known which questionnaires came back from where, some may have come through the organisations with whom copies were left, or from the direct-contact, random distribution or through the self-selection method. It was deliberately decided, not to mark the questionnaires in order to identify them because it was felt that if it was known where they came from the writer may be affected by that knowledge when analysing the data. The people who chose to be interviewed could not have remained completely anonymous, except by insisting on conducting the interview by telephone. If their circumstance of being involved in this project was known, this albeit limited knowledge could tend to affect the data analysis. A consequence which would have to be guarded against.

Couples were not interviewed because I felt that people who had been involved in committing extreme violent acts against each other, who had in most cases separated on extremely bad terms, would not see helping a student as enough incentive to face each other again. It may happen on a program such as the Oprah Winfrey Show because they are guaranteed money, instant fame and protection from each other while in the studio. Such provisions would have been beyond my logistic and economic capabilities. It would also have been a very difficult expensive and time-consuming exercise just to make the necessary arrangements.

c) Interviews with Professionals.

For the purpose of rendering fluency and immediacy to this section, I will continue with the first person reporting style.

Black Sister

One of the first organisations I contacted was Camden Black Sisters,[74] I wanted to have a view from the African female perspective and I felt that such an organisation would have a strong political analysis. The sister I spoke to, Sister Kukuwa Aba, was very polite and helpful, she confirmed that they had a professional person, Sister Ayiah Jahon, who regularly counsels some of the women and she should be most happy to help when she returned from holiday in a few days.

After several days of messages without a return call I finally spoke to Sister Ayiah. I gave her an outline of the project and asked if as a professional working in the field of caring and counselling, she would be willing to assist me. She

[74] Camden Black Sisters,(*see Appendix A for contact*)

voiced reluctance, said she did not know because its unusual for a man to be doing this kind of research. I sent her a copy of the questionnaire so she could get a better idea of where I was "coming from" before our meeting the following week.

She received the questionnaire but had "no time" to even look at it, she said. We had a very exciting meeting which lasted over two hours. She was suspicious of my motives, saying, like a typical man, I would just blame the woman, again, for being raped. This assumption she based on two statements I made. They were:

1) in any relationship where there is physical violence there will be non-physical violence[75] and

2) in every relationship each party is totally and equally responsible for what happens in the relationship.[76] At the end of our meeting, I felt she was still not satisfied that my research project would benefit her or women generally in any way. She did not call me, as she said she would.

When finally, after more messages, I caught up with her, she said the concept of *equal* responsibility was too onerous to her. We discussed for a further twenty-five minutes. I showed her that it would not be in my interest academically to present any conclusion which could not be supported by the evidence that I would be relying upon to support it and she would have an opportunity to input some of that evidence herself in her own words. She finally agreed to be interviewed, but in her individual capacity, <u>not</u> as a representative of Camden Black Sisters. I asked her to call me if there are any problems concerning our interview. She agreed that I could leave a few copies of the questionnaire at the centre.

---

[75] See also Stets,J.E., May 1990

[76] She was prepared to accept on behalf of women, full, equal responsibility for a good, harmonic relationship, but only apportioned responsibility, if any at all, for a bad relationship - even where the hostilities were mutual - because of the oppressive, unequal power relations between man and woman in society. She couldn't see how a battered woman or an abused girl can be responsible at all for being battered or abused.

I arrived ten minutes before the appointment and was told Sister Ayiah had just "stepped out for a minute". 40 minutes later someone apologised for the delay. Exactly one hour after I arrived another sister told me that Sister Ayiah was not expected back until late in the evening. She apologised for me not being informed earlier. I was not very happy to have spent nearly three hours travelling and waiting for the interview that was not going to happen. I have not had any communication directly or indirectly from "Sister" Ayiah in the past eighteen months since she treated me in such an utterly disrespectful manner.

Southall Black Sisters

The question of me being a man arose again when I called Southall Black[77] Sisters[78](SBS) in a bid to get an Asian women's perspective on the issue. I saw a woman called Sadhana Issar representing SBS on a TV talk show about the oppression of women in the Asian community and I wanted to see whether the information they receive is any different from that received by other people in their situation. She told me that they did not have any time to help. It was not until a few days later when someone else told me **they don't deal with men**, that I finally realised what was the reason for such a strong, unyielding, uncompromising force behind the negative response.

Ms. Issar denied the rumour, but admitted that they do not allow men unto their premises because the women who use the building have been brutalised by men and the last thing they would want to see is another man in a place where they are supposed to be safe - in any case, she accepted that there

---

[77] This is not a group of African women as one would expect, but Asian women who, politically, identify themselves as "Black" and "Sisters", in keeping with the now established tradition of every oppressed non-African group cashing in on the advances made through the struggles of the African nation.

[78] Southall Black Sisters, (*see Appendix A for contact*)

are no reasons why we could not meet elsewhere if she were willing to give an interview. As far as the questionnaire was concerned they could not help but if I wanted I could put my request in writing and send a copy of the questionnaire and the committee would consider it at their next meeting and contact me. This I did (*see Appendix E*). I called several times over six weeks until finally I spoke to Ms. Issar who told me categorically, that they could not help me because they do not have the time. They did not apparently, have the time even for someone to do a few minutes interview in their lunch break, on the telephone.

Everyman Centre

When I spoke to Luke Daniels of the Everyman Centre,[79] an organisation which specialises in helping men - men only - who have been convicted of domestic violence or abuse he was very eager to help. I wanted to get a feel of the type of exclusive information convicted violent men were getting, as to the nature of violence, why they behaved the way they did and what could be done to prevent further violence. I gave him a few copies of the questionnaire which he mailed out to some of his ex and current clients and we met for the interview in Kennington Park.

London Marriage Guidance

When I called what I thought was Relate[80] I spoke to Claire Ridge who said they would be happy to help if I could write a letter making an official request to Ms. Jillian Walton the head of training and supervision. This I did (*see Appendix E*) and I had an interview with her at their offices. I don't know whether they were able to copy and distribute the questionnaire as I requested and expected because I have not

---

[79] Everyman Centre, (*see Appendix A for contact*)

[80] The London Marriage Guidance or LMG an affiliate of Relate(*see Appendix A for contact*)

spoken to anyone who said they had been informed through L.M.G.

Asian Women

The Asian Women's Centre[81] is another organisation I contacted whom I was unable to interview. I spoke to someone called Ms. Amrit Virdi who seemed eager to help. She said I should write a letter (*see Appendix E*) and send some questionnaires. They do not specialise in violent relationships but they do advise women in problematic relationships and, as I said in the letter, "I would expect that wherever there are problems which require third party intervention there would at least be non-physical violence". I have called several times received many promises but no interview or even a return call.

Women Against Rape

Recognising that rape is one of the most seriously destructive acts of violence any human being can commit against another, I contacted Women Against Rape[82] (WAR) to see what information they have and give to their clients on dealing with the effects of rape, its nature, causes and prevention. Each time I called (at least six times), I was told they have my message and promised that "someone" would contact me, they either deliberately refused to or were unable to give me a contact name. I have not received a single return call from them.

Hornby and Levy

In my hunt for a legal representative I was referred by several persons to Hornby and Levy, who specialise in domestic violence cases. I spoke to a Ms. King who referred me to a Ms. Kumar. After explaining the project to her and answering

---

[81] Asian Women's Centre, (*see Appendix A for contact*)
[82] Women Against Rape, (*see Appendix A for contact*)

her questions, she said it will have to be O.K.ed by Ms. Hornby. After two further reminders she said don't call her, she would call me.

I am not surprised that I did not hear from her or anyone else from Hornby and Levy, their behaviour is perfectly in line with their policy of not representing any man where there are *allegations* of violence - even if the allegations are mutual, or the woman is the accused![83]

The Desk Research

consisted primarily of:

a) a review of previous research material into the information available on the nature of, causes and prevention of relationship violence and how this information is communicated to couples in violent relationships. On-line bibliographic sources Volnet, ASSIA, were searched as well as hard copy bibliographic sources such as the library's periodicals listings.

b) reviews of relevant audio-visual material[84]

c) an overview of current ongoing research into relationship violence.

a) Review of Previous Research.

The initial searches unearthed a rather large number of books, theses, magazine articles, newspaper articles and videos on the subject of violence between couples but none were on the information needs of these couples and none were

[83] The evidence is part of a recorded conversation with a representative.
[84] McBeth,F., *Violent Treatment*, Public Eye, BBC2 TV 11.12.1992. (for example)

on the nature of, causes of, or the prevention of violence in interpersonal relationships. They were, virtually without exception, written from the perspective that the violence which occurred between spouses was male violence and that it was physical. These findings could not be accepted because of my own experiences and contradictory evidence from elsewhere.[85]

With the aid of online expert David Nicholas more searches were done. This time four promising journal items from the ERIC database were retrieved they were: "The Information Needs of Battered Women",[86] "Community Information Needs: The Case of Wife Assault",[87] "Verbal and Physical Aggression in Marriage"[88] which has already been cited, and "Test of an Argumentative Skill Deficiency Model of Interspousal Violence".[89] At a glance from the titles and abstracts, the first two appear to be repeating the old stereotype of the battered woman and the violent man but they were not dismissed because they are the only research items, out of hundreds, which chose to concentrate on the information needs of one of the partners and the community respectively and communication of information about violence, albeit a limited view of the subject. They were yet again painting a picture of unidirectional, unilateral, physical violence by men against women.

I am not denying the fact that men do physically violate women, but women are also psychologically, emotionally, spiritually and socially violated by men more often and more seriously than physically; and women also violate men on all those levels to more or less the same degree; both men and women violate children most of the time.

---

[85] Discussions with friends, colleagues and reading 'between the lines' of these research reports.

[86] Harris,R.M., 'The Information Needs of Battered Women,' *RQ,* v28 n1 fall 1988 p62-70

[87] Dewdney,P. and Harris,R.M., 'Community Information Needs: The Case of Wife Assault', *Library and Information Science Research,* v14 n1 Jan-Mar 1992 p5-29

[88] Stets,J.E., May 1990 pp501-14

[89] Infante,D.A. and others, 'Test of an Argumentative Skill Deficiency Model of Interspousal Violence', *Communication Monographs* v56 n2 Jun 1989 p163-177

The other two items look respectively at the relationship between physical violence and non-physical violence in relationships and the types of communication in relationships which may or may not lead to physical violence. These four items prove what was said in one of them by Stets that surprisingly little has been written about non-physical violence and the relationship between physical violence and non-physical violence [90]

Attempts were made to search other bibliographic sources including the library of the Tavistock Institute a specialist research and teaching organisation. Their library is out of bounds to the public but the library person did search unsuccessfully for three of the above four items.

b) Reviews of Audio-Visual Material.

Items reviewed were "The Good Father"[91], " Violent Treatment"[92], "Do Families Need Fathers?" and "Unspeakable Acts".[93]

c) An Overview of Current Research.

The VOLNET Research Directory was searched, the nearest things to finding any current research in the area of the topic were two projects which were due to be completed in 1991! (this research project was completed in the 1992-3 season) both dealing with either "battered women" or "wife abuse" with the emphasis on violent men.

---

[90] Stets,J.E., May 1990 p501

[91] Newell,M., (Dir.) and Hampton,C., (writer) *The Good Father,* Film on Four Extra, Channel 4,1986

[92] McBeth,F.,.1992

[93] Allam,F., *Unspeakable Acts,* Dir. L.Jackson, BBC community Programme Unit, BBC2 April 1993.

Data Analysis

The collected data were analysed in 2 stages as follows:

a) a preliminary analysis of the returned questionnaires which provided some factual details of questionees and also details of percentages of people whose information needs are met or not met and to what degree; what percentage admit to practising violence, claim to be victims of violence, claim to be non-violent or claim to be involved in non-violent relationships. This information was used as part of the basic background information for interviewing those individuals who had completed and returned their questionnaires. They were also used as a basis for forging some of the questions put to the professionals in the field.

b) the second stage of analysis was more comprehensive and included all data collected from both the field and desk research and a reappraisal of the marked questionnaires in relation to the relevant interview data.

Preliminary Statistical Analysis

The percentage of questionnaires completed and returned out of the total number distributed was 21% (see Charts 1- 3). This consisted of:

76% females.

20% males.

2 people did not mark female or male but one was handed in by a female so we will assume that it was female.

52% Africans (comprising 8% men, 40% women).

4% Asian women.

56% Europeans (12% men, 44% women).

One man said he was "human".

8% of the women described themselves as mixed race (African and European) and 4% said "Black British"; the same woman who did not mark female was also an African (from the Caribbean) who did not mark "African".

I did not ask this person whether the questionnaire she handed to me was actually filled in by her because I felt that she was already trying to help and it would not have been fair on her.

Some of the figures do not add up to 100% because of indeterminate genders, the fact that the "mixed race" are ascribed to their constituent parts and various other factors already mentioned.

Of the people who were employed, 87.5% were female and 12.5% was male.

29% of the unemployed were men and 57% were women.

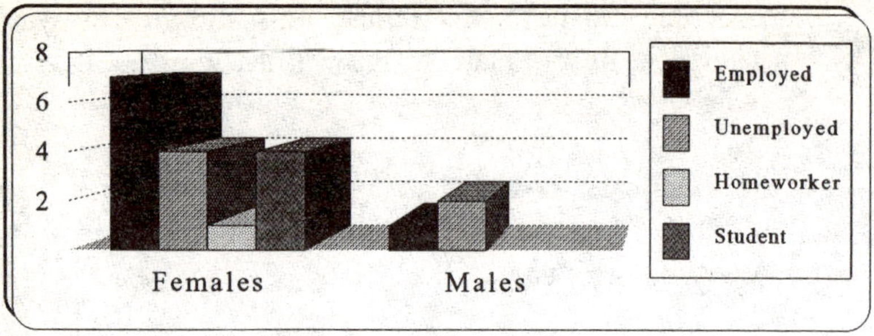

Chart 1 Occupation

A somewhat curious but serious oversight was the exclusion of "student" in the occupation category, never-the-less some women said they were students.

There was one homeworker (female).

One African man said he had never been involved in a "serious" relationship because he is celibate. It is not clear how he was using the word "celibate" which means literally "not married".[94]

Of the women who said there was no violence in any of their past or present relationships, 75% admitted that they and/or their partners had said and/or done things which, according to my definition, would in fact amount to violence.

They were either unaware of the nature of violence, found that definition of violence unacceptable or were unable to see themselves as violent, the fourth was more consistent, although she said that there is adequate information available to couples to help prevent

[94] *Collins Concise Dictionary Plus*, William Collins 1989

violence, for example "in the phone book". The indeterminate gender person, one of only two persons who were consistent in their declarations of being in "non-violent" relationships, had no definition for nor any views on forms of violence .

Of the men, 80% admitted to saying things which amount to violence while 40% admitted to saying and doing things (apart from hitting) which amounted to violence.

Of the women, 67% admitted to saying something violent while 33% admit to doing violent things (apart from hitting). 28% of women claim not to have ever said or done anything violent in their relationships.

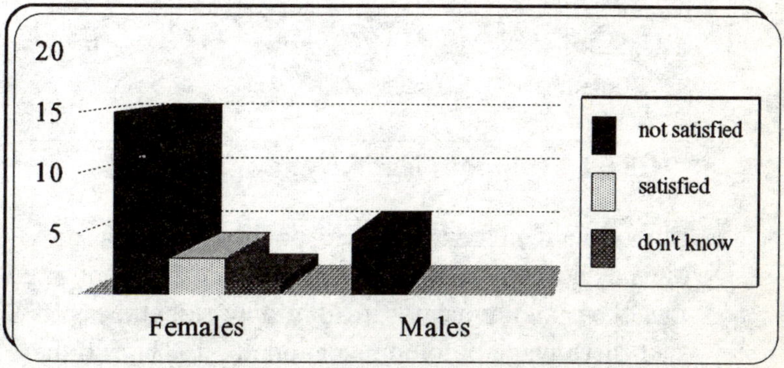

Chart 2 Adequacy of Information

12% of the people were satisfied that there is adequate information available to couples about preventing violence and resolving problems; 84% felt that there was a need for more and better information provision, while 4% didn't know.

On the question of communication, (8%) said that they and their partners communicated readily, one person also stated (wrongly as it later transpired in interview) that there was no violence in her relationships. They all never-the-less gave reasons for difficulty in communication as outside influences and lack of information.

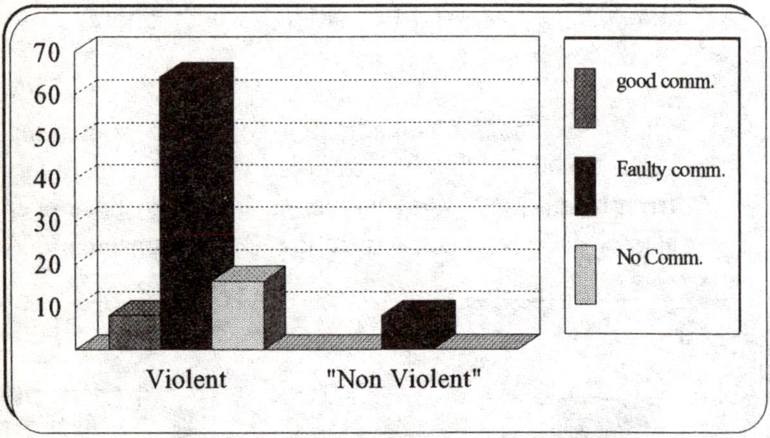

Chart 3 Communication and Violence

Eighty-eight percent of all respondents recognised violence in their relationships; 73% of them admitted that they communicated readily only sometimes; 18% said there was no communication at all, 8% said there was no communication problem. Seventy-five percent of those who did not communicate at all (16%), recognised violence in their relationships.

Of the 8% who said they had never experienced violence in their relationships, all admitted to faulty communication in the relationship which they referred to in the questionnaire or in interview.

Most of those who thought, contrary to the rest of their evidence, that there was no violence in their relationships were not available for interview.

Many of the people made some very helpful suggestions in answer to the question of what information would be useful to them and others in the future. (*See Conclusion*).

Some people communicated to me that they did not return their questionnaires because of the way the questions were structured. They felt it would have made them look stupid if they are saying at the beginning that there was no violence in their relationships but admitting in later answers that they were immersed in mutually violent relationships particularly of the non-physical kind.

Literature Review

Introduction

After an extensive search in the library at UNL and the VOLNET and ASSIA international data bases, not a single document dealing with the information needs of couples in violent relationships or the information available to them on the nature, causes and prevention of violence in relationships was found.

For the benefit of satisfying the hypothesis that the problem of relationship violence is being compounded by lack of relevant information and reinforced by the dissemination of misleading and/or false information, and in order to answer some of the questions posed, in relation to the information needs of the people in question, it was decided to look at a few representative samples of the available literature, including audio-visual material, on the subject of relationship violence.

Book and Journal Review

Marital Violence: *The Community Response*

Borkowski, Murch and Walker devote a whole chapter of "Marital Violence" to the "problems of definition".[95] They say

[95] Borkowski,M., et al p41-51

that the professionals in the fields of caring, counselling, policing and legal representation have a much broader range of definitions between them for marital violence than actual or threatened physical assault. "At first sight it seems alarming that there are so many different views about what constitutes marital violence. People may fail to appreciate how varied each other's definitions are."[96]

They also recognise that practitioners who use the definition of "persistent physical abuse" to test for violence in a relationship "practically always assumed that the violence was unilateral, perpetrated by the man on the woman."[97] and argue that there could well be partnerships where the rows and the physical abuse or 'fights' were just as persistent but *mutually inflicted*, yet seldom, if ever, were they mentioned as "persistent physical abuse". Why? Is it because of the difficulty in assessing or quantifying non-physical abuse? or is there an unwritten professional code which says that only physical abuse by men can be persistent? These questions are not answered - nor are they posed - by the authors. But it appears that one of the reasons why there is such a one-sided way of presenting reports of relationship violence is that there are people and organisations whose vested interests would be adversely affected by any idea that the women for whom they are speaking and in some cases they are being funded to provide services, may themselves be violent.

Witnessing as they obviously did, the problems caused by such unprofessional and blatant bias, it is very difficult to comprehend why they themselves chose to use as their working definition of marital violence "Threatened or actual *physical* assault by one marital partner upon the other."[98] Is it because that is what is expected as the industry standard?[99]

[96] ibid. p47
[97] Borkowski,M., et al p51
[98] Borkowski,M., et al 1983 p8
[99] Borkowski,M., et al 1983 p8

They did not have much to say about communication between the couples or information transfer between them and the professionals in the field - and did not say why.

A Father's Letters To His Daughter

In "A Father's Letters To His Daughter",[100] Brian Grant stresses the importance of communication, discussion, negotiation, in trying to limit the amount of violence and conflict that can arise out of a separation. The focus of this book is not an analysis of the nature of violence nor is it concerned with the causes of violence or the reasons for the breakdown in a relationship. It is basically a treatise on damage limitation after a couple had firmly decided to terminate a marriage.

As a former high court judge, Mr. Grant was in a very good position to advise his daughter through many long letters, how to avoid spending a lot of money in legal fees by taking a conciliatory rather than confrontational stance. His advice is basically: direct communication, and plenty of it, with the guidance of someone skilled in the art of conciliatory negotiation, is the best way to resolve the problem of who should have what and what should happen to the children. It is never-the-less an important document in the sense that the advice given is useful and if followed, could help in the prevention of violence in any relationship.

Leaving Violent Men: *A Study of Refuges and Housing for Battered Women*

Binney, Harkell and Nixon[101] show that of the women in refuges which they had investigated, ten per cent left home

---

[100]Grant,B., *Conciliation & Divorce: a father's letters to his daughter*, Barry Rose 1981
[101]Binney,V., et al, 1981

because of mental cruelty alone (sixty-eight per cent said it was one of the factors) which they declare could be "as debilitating as physical assaults, but women found it difficult to gain sympathy or help as there were no black eyes or broken bones to prove it."[102]

Mental violence not only destroys a person's confidence thereby making it virtually impossible to 'get up and go', its very intangibility and lack of corroborating evidence like physical scars makes it less likely that such a person would inform any third parties of their internal injuries.[103] It is also much more difficult to obtain funding for projects dealing with mental or non-physical violence because of the lack of physical user-friendly media material. How do you photograph a traumatised mind?

On the subject of information, they devote barely half a page to showing that refuges are the best places for a battered *woman* to get information that they should ordinarily, by right and as a matter of necessity, be getting from other agencies like Social Services, solicitors and police; information such as who pays what to your solicitor, help with legal proceedings like divorce, custody petitions and injunctions, what your Social Security rights and entitlements are, and making applications to housing associations for rehousing; not just information was given on these subjects, there were also active lobbying of particular agencies on behalf of the women; "with such help and information freely available, [at refuges] women were in a better position to make plans for their future"[104]

The opportunity to communicate with other sympathetic women about their situation was one of the major benefits of being in a refuge.[105]

[102]ibid. p4 -5
[103]ibid. p4
[104]ibid. p54
[105]ibid. p54

There is no mention of information from professionals or analytical discussions about the nature, causes or prevention of the violence which the women *suffered* from and/or *inflicted* in the relationships they were attempting to escape from.

Culture of Violence: *The Foundation of White America on Slavery and Genocide: a call for White solidarity with Black Power*

One of the objectives of this research is to investigate what effect, if any, information about differences between their cultural backgrounds and the culture of their environment may have on the amount or lack of violence in a couple's relationship. Since there appeared to be no existing research on relationship violence with a cultural analysis,[106] "Culture of Violence" by Penny Hess[107] was looked at because it promised an analysis of white culture or "White Power" as she calls it, or Global Europe[108] as it has also been called, and its relationship to violence. Ms. Hess in fact describes "white" culture as a culture of violence. She shows that White Power is based on the enslavement of Africans, the worst, most destructive of all atrocities ever committed in human history; that nothing could ever "approach the holocaust of genocide and terror that has been perpetrated by the white world in the name of Democracy, Christianity and white supremacy."[109] Not only was this genocidal attack unleashed on Africa but in addition they created and are to this day perpetuating a lie that nothing of any worth ever came out of Africa[110] A diabolical lie which

[106]Mama, A., *The Hidden Struggle: statutory and voluntary sector responses to violence against Black women in the home,* London Race and Housing Research Unit, 1989 p47
[107]Hess,P., 1991
[108]Bedeau,S.R., 'Awaiting the Global Race War:Will European unity light the fuse to a world-wide explosion of racial conflict?', *The Voice,* 6 March 1990 p68
[109]Hess,P., 1991 p3
[110]Gobineau in Banton,M., *Racial Theories*, Cambridge University Press, 1987 p48

has been recognised and exposed by many Afri-centric historians and scholars like Diop[111] and Dr. Ben.[112] But the lie could not have survived so long without the machinery, the system to perpetuate it, as Asante points out: "the European colonisation of ... land went hand in hand with the colonisation of information and knowledge".[113]

Verbal and Physical Aggression in Marriage

The question of information concerning racial/cultural background is treated quite differently by Stets in her paper "Verbal and Physical Aggression in Marriage". She uses the term "subculture of violence" to put forward an arguably racist argument that the "conditions of being black"[114] is one of the factors which supports the idea that Black people are more violent than White people because we "condone" the use of violence[115] and because of "economic strains".[116] A view which is strongly contested by Hess, herself a European, who says: "The violent nature of white people is deep."[117]

It is clear that Stets is not looking at violence in its full sense when she makes such 19th century Euro-centric statements that Africans are more violent than Europeans. It may

---

[111]Diop,C.A., *The African Origin of Civilization: Myth or Reality*, Westport, CT:Lawrence Hill, 1974.

[112]Ben-Jochannan,Y.A., *Africa: Mother of "Western Civilization"*, New York: Alkebu-Lan Books 1971.

[113]Asante,M.K., *Kemet, Afrocentricity and Knowledge*, Africa World Press, 1990 p61.

[114]Stets,J.E., May 1990 p510

[115]Stets,J.E., 1990 p505 referring to the work of criminologists Wolfgang,M.E. and Ferracuti,F., *The Subculture of Violence: Towards an Integrated Theory in Criminology*, New York, Tavistock, 1967

[116]Stets,J.E., 1990 p505 citing Cazenove,N.A., and Strauss,M.A., 'Race, Class and Network Embeddedness and Family Violence: A search for potent support systems', Journal of Comparative Family *Studies* 10: pp282-299 and Lockhart,L.L., 'A Reexamination of the Effects of Race and Social Class on the Incidence of Marital Violence: A Search for Reliable Differences', *Journal of Marriage and the Family* 49: pp603-610

[117]Hess,P., 1991 p61

appear that way to her because of the obvious and highly publicised physical manifestation of "Black on Black" violence within our community. She may be looking at the pandemic proportions of this "Black on Black" physical violence and saying 'look how violent they are, Europeans don't do that' but she is wrong, Europeans do do that, have done that, is doing that, to themselves and everyone else and above all they ***programme*** it to be done. She may not see the terror of an African community suffering the effects of constant European state violence on a continuous basis. She may not see the monstrous human rights violations of Global Europe against the rest of the world, in particular Global Africa because, if she did, she would quite clearly recognise that African people are currently and historically, the most violated people on this planet and Europeans are indeed the main perpetrators of the greater part of the violence against us.

Dr. Jack Felder shows in his book "AIDS",[118]how Global Europe has used germ warfare against Global Africa in the past with the smallpox virus and poisoning of water holes on the continent and now the deliberate invention and spread of the AIDS virus in our communities in a bid to wipe out our global population.

Although the deliberate distortion of history[119] by Europeans could, if believed by someone of African descent, cause them to have a quite negative view of themselves,[120] it does not necessarily (though it could) manifest itself in the self-destructive use of violence against a partner or acceptance of violence against themselves in a relationship.[121]That would also depend on many other elements which we will deal with later.

---

[118]Felder,J., *AIDS: United States Germ Warefare at its Best, with Documents and Proof,* Jack Felder, 1989

[119]Cush,K., *Racism in Western Culture: the Role of the Printing Press,* The Axum Foundation, 1993

[120]Woodson,C.G., 'The Miseducation of the Negro', *The Crisis,* August 1931 p266

[121]Mama, A 1989 p21

Stets later attempts what seems to be a quite unsuccessful literary somersault stating that the greater part of her assertion that Black people have a higher propensity for violence than whites can be dismissed because of "slope differences",[122] meaning that Black people are more "vulnerable" to cultural and structural variables (without clearly showing why we are more vulnerable), therefore it is "these cultural and structural factors that accounts *almost* [my italics] completely for their differences in aggression."[123]

However, neither she nor any of the other researchers she has chosen to use to substantiate her argument, take into consideration actions, in relationships which are not direct physical assault, verbal assault nor "non-verbal" assault (as she calls states of silence or non-verbal communication designed to upset a partner) actions which never-the-less can be executed and experienced as serious violations against a partner or a people. Actions such as the use or the threat of using the state machinery by a European person either covertly or overtly against the interest of their African "partner"; the use or the threat of using the same state apparatus by one African person against another, knowing that the political and legal chips are institutionally stacked against them both. Actions such as manipulation and manoeuvring of their social environment in order to disadvantage the spouse or undermine the spouse's position, are not at all taken into consideration.

The Relationship Business

In "The Relationship Business"[124] Abi Ajoni suggests that communication is the key to a good relationship; that couples should set up and run their relationship with the same

---

[122]Stets,J.E., May 1990 p511
[123] Stets,J.E., 1990 p511
[124]Ajoni,A., 1989

attention to detail as if they were running a business venture. The author suggests that from the beginning and throughout the relationship there should be communication. They should produce a working plan which is based on what each partner wants from the union and what together they both want from the union. They then set about trying to achieve the best results they can as a team by answering the questions as to who they are, what they want to achieve and the steps they will need to take or are prepared to take in order to achieve their goals. If problems arise along the way they should then look at their plan and ask themselves whether they were doing what they said they would do and if not why not, and if they are why is it not working? what needs to change in order to move forward? At each stage reassessing the situation and continuously communicating. A very sensible set of very practical steps which if followed carefully would probably take some of the uncertainty and hence a kind of masochistic excitement out of relating but it would help reduce violence.

Private Violence and Public Policy: *The Needs of Battered Women and the Response of the Public Services*

The existence, if not the seriousness, of non-physical violence was stated as part of a paragraph by Jan Pahl[125] in her introduction to "Private Violence and Public Policy: The needs of battered women and the response of the public services" where she was attempting to give meaning to her use of the term "battered wives". She says "It is important to recognise that violence can take many forms and that it includes both physical and mental assault." She goes on to say that

[125]Pahl,J.,, 1985

according to Binney, Harkell and Nixon[126] "Sixty-eight percent [of women] said that mental cruelty was one of the reasons why they left home". In the same paragraph, quoting Marsden,[127] she adds: "One definition of the problem is that 'a battered wife is a wife or cohabitee who has suffered persistent or serious *physical* assault at the hands of her partner'; however, to this definition must be added the comment of many women, that 'the ***mental battering was worse*** than the physical battering'." The rest of the entire book was devoted to talking about male *physical* violence.

According to Pahl violence against female partners is one quarter of all reported cases of violent assault currently on police files and she suggests that "the problem is more accurately described as the problem of violent husbands".[128] This figure does not take into consideration non-physical violence of *males* against their partners nor of females against their partners, since the law does not provide for criminal charges for non-physical violence in a relationship, nor does it provide for female sexual abuse in the form of female rape.[129] She suggests that the incidence of female against male partner violence is "insignificant" in relation to male against female partner violence. It may well be true that the incidence of male violence is greater than female violence, if one is looking at only "serious" physical violence which leave their visible marks but not necessarily true and certainly not insignificant when one considers "minor" physical violence like shoving and pulling, etc.[130] Further, if the statement includes non-physical violence, it is fundamentally flawed because, as far as it can be ascertained, no study has ever attempted to

---

[126] Binney, V., et al, 1981

[127] Marsden, D., 'Sociological Perspectives on Family Violence', in Martin, J., (ed.), *Violence and the Family*, Wiley, 1978

[128] Pahl, J., 1985 p5-7

[129] Allam, F., 1993

[130] Guardian Reporter, 'Do Only Women Bleed?' in *The Guardian*, 15 Jul 92

document the incidence of non-physical violence in interpersonal relationships.

The Hidden Struggle: *Statutory and Voluntary Sector Responses to Violence Against Black Women in the Home*

This book deals with a subject which has become conspicuous by its absence from the hundreds of research projects undertaken into the realms of relationship violence, that is the plight of Black women (here defined as women of African, Asian or Caribbean ancestry). Ms. Mama exposes the additional traumas experienced by these women when overt and covert institutionalised racism takes its toll during their deepest moments of crisis as they try to escape from sometimes life-threatening domestic situations. Unfortunately she takes the same line as all the other writers in her definition of domestic violence as almost exclusively male against female and essentially physical. To her credit, she voices the demands of "Black" feminists that race, religion and culture be incorporated into the analysis of violence against women.

Although it is stated clearly at the outset that they were going to deal with both the physical and emotional aspects of violence, the conclusion that "*violence* is much more often inflicted on women by men and seldom the other way round ..." [131] proves otherwise since there is no mention of any records of information showing how much emotional violence is unleashed by either party.

Other important factors of omission of this report are:

a) that it made no attempt to ascertain the causes of relationship violence

---

[131]Mama, A., 1989 p303

b) although it recommends that the community be informed on the nature of domestic violence,[132] five pages on the "nature" of violence looked more at external influences that may trigger male aggression than to any analysis of the myriad of ways in which people are or can be violated.[133]

Do Only Women Bleed?

This is one document which seems to fly in the face of recent media statements about domestic violence and supports the idea that men are also violated and abused by their female partners. Contrary to the one-sided media presentation of the helpless, powerless, abused and battered wife, this article appeared in The Guardian of 15 July 1992 entitled "Do Only Women Bleed?".[134] It heralds the opening of the first American shelter for battered men and says that research carried out in the USA between 1975 and 1991 shows that wives physically assault their husbands slightly more often than husbands physically assault their wives! It recognises that the statistics do not show the *extent* of injury sustained - which is likely to be much worse for women - nor does it show the exact "incidence" of assaults. The author suggests that women's *tolerance* of abuse can lead to a "climate of violence", (where violence is defined as physical assault), which may contribute to wife-battering. It also observes that many American women see the provision of services for battered men as an unwelcomed backlash against their efforts to protect women against male violence.

---

[132] Mama, A., 1989 p317
[133] Mama, A., 1989 pp299-303
[134] Guardian Reporter, 15 Jul 92

This article does not give any indication whether there was a cultural or racial breakdown of the people for whom the refuge was intended.

A Shame and a Disgrace

Other documents which touch on the subject of violence against men, like the 1990 article by Sandra Horley entitled "A Shame and a Disgrace"[135] generally poo-poo or ridicule the idea that already scarce resources should be wasted on men who abuse women. Which points up a hitherto denied fact, that funding and resources are the key motivating factors for some of the "professionals" in the battered wives industry.

Battered Women: *A Psychological Study of Domestic Violence*

From Roy's preface to this book, her declared intention to "explore the many aspects" and show that a "broader understanding of the dynamics" of the problem of domestic violence is of necessity, was promising.[136] But, yet again, they were dealing with physical violence not non-physical violence, as the words "psychological study" tended to suggest. However it does contain an interesting piece by Steinmetz[137] in which she dismisses the idea that women are socially conditioned not to use physical violence that's why they are verbally aggressive and men are physically violent; she contends that women are equally as likely to use physical violence as men, and citing Levinger,[138] states that women are three times as likely to

[135]Horley, S., "A Shame and a Disgrace" in *Social Work Today* (41), 21 Jun. 1990, 16-17
[136]Roy,M., (Ed.) 1977 pxi
[137]Steinmetz,S.K., p68 in Roy,M., (Ed.) 1977 pp63-72
[138]Levinger,G., "Sources of Marital Dissatisfaction Among Applicants for Divorce" in Steinmetz,S.K., p68 in Roy,M., (Ed.)1977 pp63-72.

complain of verbal abuse than men and men are hardly likely to report physical battery by women.

Contrary to the belief that men are the abusers of children,[139] which has been used to justify the Global European practice of automatically placing children with their mother - or any woman - instead of their father, she says "child abusers are more likely to be women", resulting in women being historically the "prime perpetrators of infanticide".[140] It makes logical sense to expect that if the pressures of living starts to take its toll on a woman she will express her anger and frustration on the nearest person or people to her which is usually the children.

Steinmetz goes on to say that men and women hit each other equally, with or without objects, however, the greater degree of physical injury sustained by women in non-homicidal fights is due to the greater strength and size of men generally; but ***women's use of weapons tends to equalise the damage potential*** *resulting in men and women committing "similar amounts of spousal homicide".*[141]

In dealing with the issue of **prevention** Steinmetz dismisses two equally redundant ideas:

> 1) aiding husbands to fulfil the "male role" of economic provider which basically serves to reinforce the inequality within the relationship by subscribing to the idea that a woman's welfare is a man's responsibility and she is therefore his property
>
> 2) giving wives martial arts training before they enter the marital "arena" thereby raising the level of destructiveness to one where each party decides that for

---

[139]Woodcraft,E., Channel 4, 3.12.1992
[140]Steinmetz,S.K., p68 in Roy,M., (Ed.)1977 pp63-72
[141]Steinmetz,S.K., p69 in Roy,M., (Ed.)1977 pp63-72

its own safety a gun would make the best arbiter in any argument.

Instead she suggests a "two-pronged attack on the problem":[142]

1) the immediate short-term provision of protection for the battered spouse of either gender (I expect, whether physically or non-physically battered)
2) the long-term re-education of all family members beginning with the youngest from childhood.

Audio-Visual Review

The Good Father

In "The Good Father" Bill is angered by the fact that his son's mother moved her boyfriend into his flat immediately after he walked out on them. After witnessing the pain of another man, Roger, crying for his child who was stolen by the child's mother, he helps Roger to get legal custody of the child on account of the mother's lesbianism. There doesn't seem to be any physical violence in the history of either of the relationships but never-the-less the violence is so thick and strong, the rage, the pain, the terror can almost be felt by the observer. There are no statements as to the causes of the violence nor any suggestions of solutions, except for one scene where Roger reads in jest an article by his wife who depicts the "new woman" as a rooftop sniper and states that

[142] Steinmetz,S.K., p70 in Roy,M., (Ed.)1977 pp63-72

"fundamentally, men are inferior" and biologically defective in relation to women.

Such a concept can sound very nice to a woman who has been told all her life that she was fundamentally and biologically inferior to men but according to the principle of the "duality of the one", neither man nor woman is inferior or superior to the other, each is perfect in her or his own right and therefore supreme. When they come together to create a third entity, the relationship, the contribution of both are of equal value because without either there is no relationship.

Violent Treatment

For all intents, Violent Treatment is yet another expose on physical violence as meted out to the woman by the man. It shows attempts to solve the problem by trying to "cure" the man of his bad ways, as if his actions came about in a vacuum, without any input from society or the person he was interacting with. The most significant statement was: "Instead of tackling the causes, the problem of domestic violence is simply shut away. Men here [*in prison for the crime of domestic violence*] find their beliefs only reinforced, especially that the woman played a part in provoking them."[143]

Do Families Need Fathers?

The title of this film suggests that a father is an accessory that is tacked on to a family which is essentially, a mother (no question of whether a family needs a mother) and some children (again no question of whether a family needs

[143]McBeth,F., 1992

children). The overall attitude and comments of the presenter and the contents of the documentary suggests a negative answer.

It starts out by saying that men are powerful and women are powerless; that all victims of marital assault are women, all perpetrators of domestic violence (equated as physical violence) are men, a quarter of all violent assault is domestic violence; it refutes a judge's statement that there may be reasons why a person commits a violent act; ridicules the suggestion that there may be violence between the parties because, they suggest, it is not "between the parties" it is from the man.

They gave no mention as to the probable causes, nor to the possibility that there might be some other forms of violence in the relationships observed, other than male physical violence, nor to any ideas of how to prevent violence in future. This is the kind of programme which, by its own violence of blatant deliberate lies, helps to increase rather than decrease the level of violence between men and women. Men and women who know the truth and desire harmony between the sexes, will be angry enough to want to do some damage to those who produced the garbage; men and women who know but want the war to continue will be very happy that another blow has been struck on their behalf; men who don't know the truth but know their own experiences will become more confused and disorientated but will never-the-less be more determined to exercise this power that they are supposed to have; women who don't know the truth but know their own experiences will redouble their efforts to win each battle while at the same time retaining the right to play the role of powerless, battered victim for as long as it appears to be profitable.

Unspeakable Acts

Shortly before completion of the original report, "Unspeakable Acts" was aired. It revealed that not enough information is available on the incontrovertible fact that, contrary to popular belief and media myths, women do commit rape, and do abuse children. It was also said that because female sexual abuse is far, far less than male sexual abuse it is "dangerous" to expose its existence by discussing it publicly. Yet it was admitted that not enough research has been done to establish the extent of female sexual abuse. It was also pointed out that statistics contradict the "cycle of abuse" theory, because women are more likely to be abused yet, supposedly, less likely to abuse. The theory states that people who had been abused as children invariably became abusers themselves because it was discovered that a large percentage of abusive men had been found to be abuse victims as children. So what becomes of the majority of girls who are supposed to be abused by men when they grow to be women?

Conclusion

Although there are large numbers of books, articles, videos, research documents and films on relationship violence or, as some would too narrowly call it, "domestic violence", "marital violence", or tendentiously, "wife battering", "battered women" or "wife abuse", there is very little information available on the nature, causes or prevention of violence between couples or the information needs of couples in violent or seemingly non-violent relationships. Not only are these narrow or tendentious terms used to describe interpersonal violence, the definitions applied to these terms in the face of overwhelming evidence to the contrary, suggest unfair bias in favour of people who may not ordinarily, appear to use physical violence against their partners but may persistently employ indirect or "minor" physical attacks, psychological, social, spiritual or emotional violence.

The definition of violence was more of a problem than was anticipated because of the way other writers have focused on the physical aspect, virtually eliminating any suggestion that violence could include anything that is not physical force.

The project itself was a daunting task, but it was made more difficult by the questionable behaviour of the person or persons at the university who removed the publicity posters from the walls and those, including lecturers, who actively campaigned against the idea of me researching this project without "consultation" with them. Why in hell should I have to consult with anyone who was not directly connected with the project, such as the convenor of the module. As is clear from all the publicity leaflets, they were free to approach me directly either with criticisms or better still with information which they thought would make the project better. They obviously had no intention of helping.

Why is it that Europeans generally get so upset when an African person decides to do something which they did not prescribe? It is a very common European ailment which I presume, is based on their fear that any independent action by any African person or group could be the catalistic action in an inevitable Global European cataclysm.

The uncooperative, negative attitudes of some of the "professionals" who were contacted has resulted in there being no information on the quality, quantity and type of information communicated exclusively to and from women on the nature, causes and prevention of violence. It also resulted in there being less data on the information needs of women who belong to African women's, Asian women's or multi-ethnic women's groups. This has impacted on the information I was able to access and present on the question of how differences in the cultural/racial backgrounds of a couple and their environment affect their relationship and their information gathering ability; how the quality and quantity of information available to them about each others culture and history affects the level and type of violence in their relationship. Due to the fact that there is so much information available on the subject, written by women, some of whom are professionals in the field, for women, from a women's perspective, it is possible to surmise that the information most of the professionals would give to their clients would be similar to some of those reviewed in the Literature Review section.

One consolation was the very clear and concise interview contribution from "Mary" (whose identity, unfortunately, cannot be revealed), on the information needs of women in the refuge where she worked in Australia. Though she revealed that the policy of the refuge said women were responsible for their own lives, the workers did not follow through with that policy to show the women how they were also responsible for the part of their lives which was spent in a violent situation. Instead, their attitude was very similar to that of the women who came to the refuge to "get away from the violence"; their attitude was that "the violence" was the man. Of course the examples she gave confirms that those men were extremely violent people who had used extreme physical violence against these women. But though the women were "responsible for their own lives" there is no indication that they were in any way responsible for the outcome of their interaction with those men - or that they had anything to do with it at all. I don't suppose that the situation is much different or that the information given to women in women's refuges is any different in England or anywhere else.

As is evident from the overwhelming number of female volunteers, and the abundance of data on and from the women's perspective, there was enough data available to make informed, conclusive judgements in relation to the aims, objectives and purpose of this project. The disproportionate number of female to male volunteers may be evidence of support for the generally held view that women are victims and men are violent, but it could equally be evidence of support for Steinmetz's statement that men are hardly likely to report being battered, whereas women are three times more likely to complain of abuse. Freeman puts the figure at eleven to one.[144]

It is important to note that not only African and Asian professionals were reluctant to support this research project, even though more persistent attempts were made to interview a

---

[144]Freeman, M.D.A.,"What do we know of the Causes of Wife Battering?" in *Family Law* p197

representative of the African professional community. Hornby and Levy are a private European company and Women Against Rape is a funded organisation under European women's control. All those who refused to co-operate had only one thing in common: the fact that they were women.

That fact throws up some very interesting and disturbing questions. Is it that women across the board have no desire to see or hear men's views in the violence industry? If that is the case how do they expect to resolve the problem of gender conflict without involving men? A problem between two people cannot be resolved by only one of them. True, one can unilaterally remove herself or himself from the other or their relative power positions can be reversed by trickery, stealth, force etc. but the problem will still remain and may even get worse, if they are not both involved in its resolution.

Or is it that they don't want anyone, man or woman, asking questions about the type of information they give to other women on the subject of relationship violence? If what they say and what they do are unashamedly correct and above board, why do they want to hide it? Why are they so afraid of scrutiny by an un-'supervised', non-'consulting', investigative man? Why did they all refuse to talk to me? Why? Those are questions only the women themselves can answer. I hope after reading this book they will volunteer some answers.

It could be that they were just being themselves, women who fear independent male intervention in a virtual female monopoly and simply Europeans or Asians who fear independent African action.

It appears to have made no difference to the African professional that the researcher was African, only the fact that he was a man. Some African women in the women's aid industry seem to have little or no regard for African men. They appear to have less affinity with African men than with European women - if any at all.

There are a few men who, for reasons known only to themselves, actively support these women in their anti-male campaigns and use every opportunity to cut another man down to their size. They are sometimes called "New Men". The African New Man doesn't just support African women against African men, they also support European women against African men. They do this even in an environment where the balance of power is clearly in favour of the European woman.

There are, on the other hand, some women who understand that we are all responsible for what we do and the consequences of what we do; who are not prepared to lie down, play dead and blame men for everything. They include dynamic women such as Sister Nzinga quoted earlier, who said that women are in fact responsible for what they do and are equally responsible for what happens in their relationships.

There are some very dangerous and unprincipled people in our society, apart from politicians and other such crooks, who, instead of helping people to resolve their problems, specialise in misinforming and misleading their clients into positions where the clients are more likely to experience greater conflict and confrontation and thereby increase their clients' dependency on the advice they are selling.

Some of these people pretend to be helping women but most make no pretence of covering up their own hatred of men. All they appear to be interested in is dumping their baggage of hate and fear on some unsuspecting woman, who may or may not have a justifiable grievance and using her as cannon fodder to terrorise a man, any man. It wouldn't matter to these women whether the woman and her children come out worse at the end of their professional "help", at least they would have struck another blow against 'male supremacy', 'patriarchy' and 'male chauvinism'.

The lack of input from a legal representative does not detract from the well documented, general opinion that information on the law and relationship violence is dismally inadequate, as are the laws themselves, both as preventative methods and remedies.

So, have the questions been answered? This book goes some way towards confirming the stated observations and at least throws into the information arena a broader debate on relationship violence. It throws light on the relationship between the communication of information on the nature of violence and the causes and prevention of violence in interpersonal relationships. The hypothesis that there is not enough relevant information and that much of the available information is misleading or erroneous is proven, not only by what the people say in the questionnaires and interviews, "I didn't know that was violence ... I've never hit anyone ... that means we're all violent, doesn't it?", but also by the media themselves who, with few exceptions, see only one side of the argument, are generally not interested in causes or prevention, and have less regard for solutions than sensation.

It is also clear that the majority of available information tends to depower women. Women are lead to believe that they are not responsible for what happens in their relationships, neither the positive nor the negative because the man is the power, the provider, the driving force. Never the less, most women are prepared to accept that they are at least partly responsible for the positive, pleasant aspects but find great difficulty taking responsibility for the negative, bad bits.

It is clear that most of the female respondents believe that the causes of their relationship problems and the violence is nothing to do with them. They see the causes as being some irreconcilable, external forces such as patriarchy or "*his* instabilities" thereby removing or at least masking, their responsibility for affecting or changing their situation.

Most male respondents on the other hand tended to accept some responsibility, along with their partners, for the violence but some were quick to point out that their actions were due to factors entirely beyond their control such as child abuse.

The same information given to women and communicated to men at the same time, tends to remove men's responsibility for their actions by ascribing the cause of their behaviour to forces outside and beyond them or to an immutable, internal biological determinant such as male hormone, thereby also, effectively depowering men.

The evidence presented here shows that contrary to popular belief women hit men at least as often as men hit women; that because men do greater damage without weapons women make greater use of weapons as an equalising agent.

On the question of communication and information, the evidence is overwhelming that lack of communication between couples, further exacerbated by misleading information and/or lack of relevant information has a detrimental effect on a relationship. The statistics show that there is a direct correlation between the amount of violence in a relationship and the quantity and quality of communication between the parties. Also, lack of understanding of each other's cultural backgrounds tends to create more misunderstanding, friction, mistrust, insecurity and violence.

In a society founded on principles of falsehood and deception, it is quite "normal" for couples to remain unaware of the true characters of their partners, their economic, social, political etc. backgrounds, their aims, objectives, aspirations, beliefs and affiliations. From their very first meeting where one or both of them present false pictures of themselves, they try to build a relationship on quicksand. With a cocktail of violence and ignorance they tend to stagger through to the bitter, usually destructive end.

Many people seem to think that violence is just physical assault, and from the evidence of this research, there is little knowledge or understanding of its other, less tangible, non-physical aspects. Though the evidence suggests that non-physical violence is by far more destructive and more difficult to treat than physical violence, it is physical assault on the person, primarily man against woman, preyed on by the media and those looking for financial support for their pet projects, which draws all the attention.

There are very few legal remedies for non-physical violence. There is no recognition legally, of the term non-physical violence. Even though the police and other agencies are coming to an understanding and acceptance of the dangers and seriousness of physical "domestic" violence, there is a complete blank as far as the non-physical aspects of violence are concerned - even though they are in many ways far, far more serious and "devastating", as Jillian Walton said "In a long-term sense it's often emotional violence that is the most insidious and the most destructive to the person".

I am not trying to insinuate that women are more dangerous because they are forced to utilise non-physical violence more effectively than men. I am actually trying to show that a *person* is more at risk and has less prospects of protection from the non-physical aspects of violence that is unleashed on them than the physical.

Because of the way society is structured, the woman starts off at a disadvantage to begin with. When she is actually confronted by this person who is usually bigger and stronger physically, he doesn't have to utilise his physical advantage because there is a body of institutions behind him such as the law, the church, social traditions, etc. which allow him to terrorise her mentally, emotionally and spiritually with virtual impunity. But there are legal sanctions which she can use if he *hits* her or causes her any physical injury. Which tends to make physical assault not his first but his last option, with the constant threat that it can - and in many cases will - be used.

She also, uses non-physical terrorism with legal impunity but risks physical retaliation from the man with greater force as the final arbiter. This risk is sometimes used to her advantage as a means of gathering support for her position when all else fails. So the objective of both parties in violent encounters is to avoid physical violence at all costs, unless they feel, each for their own reason that it is the only way left to settle the argument. This could explain why, according to Steinmetz, physical violence can so rapidly escalate to the use of weapons and deadly force.

The professionals recognised and commented on state violence, but socio-political violence, although experienced by most, was recognised by a small minority of the interviewees.

On the question of information concerning historical/cultural differences, the evidence suggests that the dissemination of erroneous and misleading information is widespread. The removal of historical data and its replacement with the lie, itself a violation of the rights of a people; the suppression of relevant information due to bias on the part of some Eurocentric researchers, information and media professionals against certain groups of people, in particular African people, can help to create an atmosphere that is conducive to extreme forms of physical violence and social upheaval.

Unless all forms of violence are taken into consideration, one cannot reasonably and fairly come to a conclusion that any sector of society is more violent than the others. Especially so in a society which, according to Hess, was built on and is still based on violence: "It is the pedestal of world humanity that has given us both our affluence and our culture of violence."[145] More honest research needs to be undertaken into the nature of violence and its relationship with the historical/cultural environment before drawing any conclusions about the aggressiveness of any group of people based on one or two aspects of a very wide range of violent behaviours.

It is a very well documented fact that Global European culture is a violent culture. The way they have used *physical* violence in their attempt to dominate or eliminate every other people they have ever come into contact with has been documented by scores of historians including ben-Jochannan, Clarke, Diop, Rogers, etc. But I am not satisfied that that alone qualifies them for the "most violent nation" title/status; it would be as wrong as saying that African people are more violent because we use more physical violence against *each other* than Europeans do.

It would be the same as saying a particular supermarket has more *cereals* than any other supermarket in the area because it has more *cornflakes* than the other supermarkets. Your statement could be true; it could also be false, but it is prejudicial. Until you know exactly how much of each different type or brand of cereal each supermarket has the statement is misleading. Supermarket 'A' might have so little of the dozens of other cereals on the market that its total amount of cereals is negligible compared to the supermarket which carries only two or three boxes of every type of cereal available.

I am not saying in this book that Europeans are naturally more violent than Africans and I am not saying that they are not because they have obviously used and caused more violence than any other nation in history. Until the necessary research has been undertaken, I have to at least see the

[145]Hess,P., 1991 p61

possibility that Africans or any other nation given the same environmental/historical circumstances could have or might have, behaved in a similar manner to Europeans.

It is ultimately, not profitable to the majority of men and certainly less so to a greater majority of women, to be told that women are inherently powerless or inherently defenceless. It is convenient for a great many men to live this lie, it is also convenient for too many women to live and encourage the same lie for their own short-term gain, e.g. as champions of a "defenceless", "powerless" majority. Such a lie will continue to appear to be truth until women, men, children, individuals, oppressed minorities and oppressed majorities all over the world, come to understand and accept, that the only way any entity can exercise power over another is with the consent of the oppressed, a concession which can at any time be withdrawn thereby leaving the oppressor powerless - except with the ability then to exercise power over self.

It is in the interests of those who benefit from oppression for all oppressed people to see themselves as permanent victims rather than as independent, self-determinate people who have the power to change their circumstances for the better.[146]

It is in the interest of the oppressed and victimised to recognise that they are also involved in the process of their oppression or victimisation and that they are equally responsible, with all the forces which interact to arrive at that outcome, for what happens to them. In other words they are responsible for their own oppression and equally they are responsible for their own liberation. They are equally responsible, with all the other parties involved, for their relationships and they are responsible, equally with their partners, for the harmony or disharmony in their relationships. After all, there would be no relationship at all without either partner.

---

[146]Rodgerson,G. and Wilson,E., (eds.), 1991 p37

Recommendations

These recommendations are not in any order of importance but those stressing self help take priority.

Every person who believes they know should inform others freely and let them use the knowledge as they see fit.

On meeting new people, new relationships, we must be honest about who we are and not try to impress by pretending to be someone or something other than what we are.

Men and women should meet each other regularly and exchange information on their experiences of violence.

More communication of ideas and principles of self determination, teaching by example, from person to person, parent to child and most importantly child to parent; it is time for parents to listen to the ideas of their children who may not have been totally conditioned to act against their own interests yet.

More people should be willing to take their lives into their own hands to change society for the benefit of all who live in this beautiful world of ours.

More research is needed in the area of interpersonal communication and violence to determine if, how, and/or when faulty communication becomes violent behaviour.

More research needs to be undertaken into the nature of violence and how information or lack of information, on its relationship with the historical/cultural environment affects couples interacting with each other.

Children, men and women must all be informed through all the various media, by whatever means of communication that violence is a denial of their basic human rights.

In order to have harmony in our relationships we need to go through the five stages of the healing process after suffering the damaging effects of violence. They consist of: 1) damage assessment, 2) guilt acknowledgement, 3) expressions of regret, 4) compensation/reparation and 5) reconciliation/separation.

New means of formulating laws need to be implemented where all the people are involved most of the time.

New research needs to be undertaken to determine if and how the law could be used to prevent violence and protect violated partners paying particular attention to the "most destructive" aspect, non-physical violence.

People should be informed generally, about the relevance of all laws concerning families and personal relationships and given the opportunity to repeal or change those which are understood to be violent, inspire or create an atmosphere of violence in relationships.

A comprehensive analysis of violence, geared towards self-empowerment and prevention, must be demanded by those who care and undertaken by those who can; it is urgently needed.

Those who *profess* concern with finding solutions to the problem of relationship violence should take every opportunity, regardless who presents it, to discuss the issue openly and honestly, (because oppression flourishes in secrecy and suppression[147]) involving the violator as well as the violated as independent, fully self-empowered individuals, totally responsible for all the consequences of their actions - positive and negative, good and bad. If the professionals themselves are not strong enough to face the truth or support the creation of an environment where truth can be expressed, it is difficult to imagine how they will be able to inform and inspire their clients to achieve greater self-empowerment. Hopefully, this research and others like it will help.

---

[147]Girodias,M., *The Obscenity Report,* Olympia Press, 1971. p15-31

PART III

Appendices

Appendix A

Sample of Organisation Addresses

Afro-Caribbean Mental Health Association, 35 Electric Avenue, Brixton, London SW98JP Tel: 0171 737 3603

Asian Women's Centre, 307 Plumstead High Street, London S.E.18 1JX. Tel: 0181 3116200

British Association for Counselling, 1 Regent Place, Rugby CV21 2PJ. Tel: 01788 578328, fax: 01788 562189.

Camden Black Sisters, 2C Falkland Road, Kentish Town, London NW5 2PT. Tel: 0171 284 3336.

Everyman Centre, 30A Brixton Road, London SW9 6BU. Tel: 0171 793 0255.

London Marriage Guidance, 76A New Cavendish Street, London W1M 7LB. tel: 0171 580 1087.

NAFSIYAT, 278 Seven Sisters Road, Finsbury Park, London N4 2HY. Tel: 0171 263 4130

Relate, Herbert Grey College, Little Church Street, Rugby CV21 3AP Tel: (01788) 73242

Southall Black Sisters, 52 Norwood Road, Southall, Middlesex, UB2 4DW Tel: 0181 571 9595

Training For Life, 27 Clarence Crescent, London SW4. Tel: 0181 671 2777.

Women Against Rape, Kings Cross Women's Centre, POBox 287 LondonNW6 5QU Tel: 0171 837 7509

Women's Aid Federation, England, P.O.Box 391 Bristol BS99 7WS.

Appendix B

Sample of Publicity Leaflets

Relationship Violence

Have you ever experienced any form of violence in a relationship? or do you know anyone who has either been violated or had violence committed against them? If the answer is yes, you may be able to help.

As a graduate student at the University of North London, I have chosen Relationship Violence as my final year dissertation research project. I am looking for people who may be willing to complete a questionnaire on the subject. The research will also include a limited number of interviews with some of the people who have completed the questionnaire.

If you would like to help, please pick up a questionnaire from Margery in the admin. office, on the ground floor at Ladbroke House, fill it in and either post it to me at the address at the bottom of this page or return it to the office. Your anonymity is guaranteed and no names (real or otherwise) will be mentioned in the final report.

Thanking you in advance for your most valued co-operation.

To the person who has been **tearing down these posters,**

It may well be your intention, but please note that you are violating my rights and causing me serious problems. Might I suggest that if you have a problem, either with me or the content of the poster, that you contact me about it so we could discuss your problem.

Appendix C

Sample of Questions to Professionals

Questions to professionals

1) a) What kind/type of information do you give to your clients about the nature of violence i.e. how do you define it to your clients?

b) Do you make distinction between physical and non-physical violence?

c) Which would you say is the worse to deal with on a professional level

2) a) How would you say your clients define violence?

b) Do they make any distinction between physical and non-physical violence?

c) If yes, which in their opinion was worse?

3) a) What do you feel are the main causes of violence?

a1) Is communication or the lack of it a factor?

b) What do you tell your clients about the causes of violence

c) What advice do you give as to the prevention or discontinuation of violence in a relationship?

4) a) Do you think violence of any kind can ever be justified?

b) If yes, under what circumstances?

c) If no, why not?

5) a) Do you believe that couples generally have enough information available to them that will help prevent violence?

b) If not, what suggestions would you make?

6) Knowing the objectives of this project, is there anything you would like to add which you feel has been overlooked but would be of value to the research?

7) Finally, thank you very much for your co-operation. Would you have any objections to me quoting you and using your name? Thanks.

Appendix D

Sample of Questions to Volunteers

Relationship Violence

Questions to Volunteers

1) What would you say was the cause of violence between you?

2) What part did communication, or the lack of it, play in creating or avoiding problems?

3) Do you believe you now have enough information of the correct type to have harmonious relations in future? If yes what are they, if no, why not?

4) What obligations, if any, do you think society has, to inform individuals and couples about relationship violence?

Thank you very much for your help if there is anything which you feel has not been covered but could be of value to the research project, please feel free to add, and if at any time in the future you feel that I could be of assistance to you please do not hesitate to call me, I will be more than happy to help in any way I can. Thanks.

Appendix E

Sample of Letters to Organisations

Ms. Sadhana Issar
Southall Black Sisters
52 Norwood Road
Southall
Middlesex UB2 4DW

5 March 1993

Ref.: Relationship Violence

Dear Ms.Issar

Further to my telephone conversation with you today, this letter is an official request to interview one of your advisors as a professional working in the field of advising/counselling/providing aid for women experiencing difficulty in their relationships.

As an undergraduate Social Science student at the University of North London, I have chosen Relationship Violence as my final year dissertation project. It is research into the information needs of couples in relationships with physical and non-physical violence.

Part of this research requires interviews with professionals to find out the quality, quantity and type of information which is given to their clients on: (a) the nature of violence, (b) what to do about its presence and (c) how to prevent it from occurring or recurring and in their relationships. I know that your organisation does not deal exclusively with violent relationships but you do advise women in problematic relationships and I would expect that wherever there are problems which require third party intervention there would at least be non-physical violence. I would greatly appreciate your assistance or one of your colleagues as an interviewee in your professional capacity.

As mentioned, I am also looking for people who may be willing to complete a questionnaire (1 copy enclosed but if you need more please phone) on the subject of relationship violence. The research will also include a limited number of interviews with some of the people who have completed the questionnaire. If you know of any clients who may be able to assist in this way your help will be further appreciated.

Sincerely

S.R.Bedeau

Appendix F

Questionnaire with Covering Letter

ATTENTION: **Reader**

SUBJECT: Bsc. Social Science Degree - Research Report

Dear Reader,

I am a [under]graduate student at the University of North London and the following questionnaire is part of my final year research project. The research will also include a limited number of interviews with some of the people who have completed this questionnaire.

If you would not mind being interviewed, please write a name (it does not have to be your real name) and a means of contacting you, e.g. your address and/or your telephone number, on the back of the last page and return the completed questionnaire to me at the address at the bottom of this page.

Your anonymity is guaranteed and no names (real or otherwise) will be mentioned in the final report.

Thanking you in advance for your most valued co-operation.

Yours Sincerely,

S.R. Bedeau

Questionnaire

Relationship Violence

Research questionnaire into the Information Needs of Couples in
Relationships with Physical and Non-Physical Violence

Please fill in the spaces, tick boxes, where appropriate.

Age : a) under 25 b) 26 - 35 c) 36 - 45 d) over 45
Sex : a) female b) male
Occupation :
a) employed b) self employed
c) unemployed d) homeworker
Racial/Cultural background:
a) African b) Asian c) European
d) other (please specify)

1) Have you ever been involved in a personal relationship with anyone (of either the opposite sex or the same sex)?
a) yes (go to next question)
b) no (go to question 22)

1.1) How many times have you been involved in a personal relationship?
a) once
b) 2 - 3 times
c) 4 - 6 times
d) 7 times and over

2) Are you currently involved in a personal relationship with anyone (of either the opposite sex or the same sex) ?

a) yes (go to next question 2.1)
b) no (go to question 3.)

2.1) Is your current relationship your first?

a) yes (continue)
b) no (go to question 3)

2.2) How long have you been involved in your current relationship?

a) less than 6 months
b) 6 months to 1 year
c) 1 - 2 years
d) 3 - 4 years
e) 5 - 6 years
f) 7 - 10 years
g) 11 - 15 years
h) over 15 years

2.3) Has this involvement been:

a) continuous without breaks?
b) on and off with breaks?

2.4) Has there ever been any violence in your relationship from either side?

a) yes (go to question 3.1)
b) no (go to question 4)

3) Have you ever been involved in a relationship where there was violence from either side?

a) yes (go to question 3.1)
b) no (go to question 4)

3.1) How many of the relationships you have been involved in included violence?

a) all of them
b) most of them
c) a few of them
d) two of them
e) one of them

3.2) Are you currently in a relationship where there has been violence?

a) yes (go to question 3.3)
b) no (go to question 3.4)

3.3) How long have you been involved in this relationship?

(go to table 1 and tick one box in column 3.3)

3.4) How long did the last relationship you had which included violence go on for?

(go to table 1 and tick one box in column 3.4)

	3.3			**3.4**
a		less than 6 months	a	
b		6 months to 1 year	b	
c		1 - 2 years	c	
d		3 - 4 years	d	
e		5 - 6 years	e	
f		7 - 10 years	f	
g		11 - 15 years	g	
h		over 15 years	h	

Table 1

3.5) Has this relationship been:

a) continuous without breaks?
b) on and off with breaks during the entire period?

4) Have you ever said anything designed to or intended to cause your partner/ex-partner injury, pain, discomfort or disadvantage?

a) yes (go to question 4.1)
b) no (go to question 5)

4.1) How often have you said any of these things?

a) all of the time
b) most of the time
c) sometimes but not very often
d) rarely
e) only once

4.2) How did your partner/ex-partner react?

a) showed no reaction
b) laughed it off
c) was obviously upset but did and said nothing
d) retaliated verbally
e) retaliated physically
f) other reaction (please explain briefly)

....

....

5) Have you ever done anything (apart from hitting your partner/ex-partner) which was designed to or intended to cause your partner/ex-partner injury, pain, discomfort or disadvantage?

a) yes (go to question 5.1)
b) no (go to question 6)

5.1) How often have you done any of these things?

a) all of the time
b) most of the time
c) sometimes but not very often
d) rarely
e) only once

5.2) How did your partner/ex-partner react?

a) showed no reaction
b) laughed it off
c) was obviously upset but did and said nothing
d) retaliated verbally
e) retaliated physically
f) other reaction (please explain briefly)

....

....

6) Has your partner/ex-partner ever <u>said</u> anything which you felt was designed to or intended to cause you injury, pain, discomfort or disadvantage?

a) yes (go to question 6.1)
b) no (go to question 7)

6.1) How often did your partner/ex-partner say such things?

a) all of the time
b) most of the time
c) sometimes but not very often
d) rarely
e) only once

6.2) How did you react?

a) showed no reaction
b) laughed it off
c) you were upset but did and said nothing
d) you retaliated verbally
e) you retaliated physically
f) other reaction (please explain briefly)

....

....

7) Has your partner/ex-partner ever done anything (apart from hitting you) which you felt was designed to or intended to cause you injury, pain, discomfort or disadvantage?

a) yes (go to question 7.1)
b) no (go to question 8)

7.1) How often did your partner/ex do any of these things?

a) all of the time
b) most of the time
c) sometimes but not very often
d) rarely
e) only once

7.2) How did you react?

a) showed no reaction
b) laughed it off
c) you were upset but did and said nothing
d) retaliated verbally
e) retaliated physically
f) other reaction (please explain briefly)

....

....

8) Did you or your partner/ex-partner ever impose any rules, regulations, conditions, or ultimatums on each other which were designed to, intended to or actually did restrict or dictate each other's movement or suppress their expression in any way?

(please tick one or more)

a) your partner/ex-partner always did

b) your partner/ex-partner most of the time

c) your partner/ex-partner sometimes but not often

d) you and your partner/ex-partner equally sometimes

e) you sometimes but not often

f) you most of the time

g) you always did

h) neither of you ever did

8.1) If you ticked any of a) to g), give 3 examples of the kinds of rules which were imposed.

1) ....

....

2) ....

....

3) ....

....

9) How would you define violence in your own words?

....

....

....

....

....

10) Do you believe there are any other forms of violence apart from physical violence?

a) yes (go to question 10.1)
b) no (go to question 11)

10.1) How many forms of violence can you identify?
please list:...
....
....
....

11) Whenever there was any violence in your relationship, who would you say committed it? a) your partner/ex-partner
b) you
c) both of you

11.1) What form did this violence take?
a) physical
b) emotional
c) psychological
d) social
e) spiritual

11.2) How often did violence occur?
a) all of the time
b) quite often
c) not often
d) once

12) How did you react to violence against you?
a) apologised for what you had done to cause it
b) pretended it did not happen

c) you said you deserved it anyway

d) you said he/she was wrong to treat you that way

e) you reported it to a third party (e.g. took legal action)

f) you retaliated verbally and/or physically

g) you terminated the relationship

h) other reaction (explain briefly)

....

....

13) How did your partner/ex-partner react to violence by you against her/him?

a) apologised for what they had done to cause it

b) pretended it did not happen (did nothing)

c) he/she said they deserved it anyway

d) he/she said you were wrong to treat them that way

e) he/she reported it to a third party (e.g. took legal action)

f) he/she retaliated verbally and/or physically

g) he/she terminated the relationship

h) other reaction (explain briefly)

....

....

14) How much of what has happened in the relationship can you say was good?

a) everything

b) most things

c) some things

d) very few things

e) nothing at all

14.1) Who would you say was responsible for the good things (if any)?

a) you entirely
b) you mostly
c) you and your partner/ex-partner equally
d) your partner/ex-partner mostly
e) your partner/ex-partner entirely

15) How much of what has happened in the relationship can you say was bad?

a) everything
b) most things
c) some things
d) very few things
e) nothing at all

15.1) Who would you say was responsible for the bad things (if any)?

a) you entirely
b) you mostly
c) you and your partner/ex-partner equally
d) your partner/ex-partner mostly
e) your partner/ex-partner entirely

16) Whenever there was any "problems" between you which may or may not have resulted in violence, were they resolved by: (tick one or more as appropriate):

a) calm discussion between you
b) heated argument
c) physical violence
d) arbitration/intervention from a third party (e.g. friend, relative, counsellor, legal, police)

e) doing nothing and hoping things will "blow over" with the passage of time

f) the "kiss-and-make-up" method

g) other means (please specify)

....

....

h) never resolved at all

17) Do you feel that you and your partner/ex-partner communicate(d) readily ?

a) always (go to question 17.1)

b) sometimes (go to questions 17.1 and 17.2)

c) not at all (go to question 17.2)

17.1) What do/did you talk about? (please tick one or more items)

a) sex

b) other people

c) her/his job

d) your job

e) current affairs and politics

f) T.V. programmes

g) money

h) your relationship

i) anything and everything

j) other (please specify)

17.2) Was the difficulty in communication due to:

a) your partner/ex's inability to communicate

b) your own inability to communicate

c) both of you equally

d) lack of information on the subjects at hand

e) other (please specify)

18) Do you feel that there is adequate information available to couples about preventing violence or resolving problems in their relationships?

a) yes (go to question 18.1)
b) no (go to question 18.2)

18.1) Can you give examples of some sources of such information?

....
....
....

18.2) What kind of information do you think would have been helpful to you in preventing violence in your relationship?

....
....
....
....
....

18.3) What kind of information would you like to see available to couples in future?

....
....
....

19) Have you or your partner/ex-partner ever tried to get information from outside agencies or individuals in your attempts to resolve any problems between you?

a) yes (go to question 19.1)
b) no (go to question 19.2)

19.1) What was the result?

a) the information received helped to resolve the problem

b) the information received helped but did not resolve the problem

c) the information received did not help at all

d) no information was available or obtained

e) other (please specify)

19.2) Why not?

....

....

....

....

20) Do you feel generally, that your information needs with regards relationship violence have been satisfied ? (please tick one or more items)

a) by your efforts

b) by your partner/ex-partner's efforts

c) by the level of communication between you

d) by information received from third parties

e) not resolved at all

21) How much has this relationship been typical of your other involvements in terms of the amount, type or lack of violence between you?

a) very typical

b) sort of typical

c) sort of untypical

d) very untypical

22) Is your answer to question 1.(b) because:

a) you are too young

b) you do not understand the question

c) you have a particular definition of the term "personal relationship" that falls outside the scope of this questionnaire, if so please give a brief explanation:

....

....

....

....

....

....

23) Finally, is there anything you wish to add which you feel have been overlooked and may be of use to the research? (Please use a separate sheet of paper if necessary).

Notes

Bibliography

Ajoni,A.., *The Relationship Business*, Candid Books 1989.

Akbar,N., *Chains and Images of Psychological Slavery*, New Mind Productions 1990.

Allam,F., *Unspeakable Acts,* Dir. L.Jackson, BBC community Programme Unit, BBC2 April 1993.

Aldridge,D.P., *Focussing: Black Male-Female relationships,* Third World Press, 1991

Asante,M.K., *Kemet, Afrocentricity and Knowledge,* Africa World Press, 1990.

Baron,R.A., *Human Aggression,* Plenum 1977.

Bedeau,S.R., 'Awaiting the Global Race War: Will European unity light the fuse to a worldwide explosion of racial conflict?', *The Voice,* 6 March 1990 p68.

Ben-Jochannan,Y.A.A., *Africa: Mother of "Western Civilization",* New York: Alkebu-Lan Books 1971.

Binney,V., Harkell,G. and Nixon,J., *Leaving Violent Men: A Study of Refuges and Housing for Battered Women,* Womens Aid Federation (UK) 1981.

Borkowski,M., Murch,M. and Walker,V., *Marital Violence: The Community Response,* Tavistock Publications 1983.

Campbell,A. and Gibbs,J.J., Eds., *Violent Transactions*, Basil Blackwell, 1986

Coulson,.R., *Fighting Fair: family mediation will work for you*, The Free Press 1983.

Cress-Welsing,F., *Colour Confrontation & Racism (White Supremacy)* C-R Publications, 1970

Cress-Welsing,F., *The Isis Papers: the keys to the colors,* Third World Press, 1991

Cush,K., *Racism in Western Culture: the Role of the Printing Press,* The Axum Foundation, 1993

Dewdney,P. and Harris,R.M., 'Community Information Needs: The Case of Wife Assault', *Library and Information Science Research,* v14 n1 Jan-Mar 1992 p5-29.

Diop,C.A., *The African Origin of Civilization: Myth or Reality*, Westport, CT:Lawrence Hill, 1974.

Felder,J., *AIDS: United States Germ Warefare at its Best, with Documents and Proof*, Jack Felder, 1989

Ferguson,M., *The Aquarian Conspiracy: personal and social transformation in the 1980's*, Paladin/Grafton Books 1989.

Garbino,J., Guttman,E. and Seeley,J., *The Psychologically Battered Child,* San Francisco: Josey-Bass 1986.

Gelles,R.J. and Straus,M.A., 'Determinants of Violence in the Family: Toward a Theoretical Integration,' in Wesley R. Burr, Rueben Hill, F. Ivan Nye, and Ira L. Reiss (eds.), *Contemporary Theories About the Family* (Vol.1) New York: Free Press 1979 pp549-581.

Girodias,M., *The Obscenity Report,* Olympia Press, 1971.

Grant,B., *Conciliation & Divorce: a father's letters to his daughter*, Barry Rose 1981.

Griffiths,G. & Davies,A., *Making Fathers Pay,* Public Eye BBC 2 TV 1990.

Hadley, J., 'The Terror of Domestic Violence', in *Community Care* 813, 10 May 1990, 16-17.

Hess,P., *Culture of Violence: The Foundation of White America on Slavery and Genocide: a call for White solidarity with Black Power*, Burning Spear Publications, 1991.

Homans & Satow, 'Can You Hear Me? Cultural variations in communication', in *Journal of Community Nursing*, 15.1.1982 p3-12.

Horley, S., 'A Shame and a Disgrace' in *Social Work Today* (41), 21 Jun. 1990, 16-17.

Hutchinson,E.O., *Assassination of the Black Male Image,* Middle Passage Press, 1994

Information Project for Africa, *Excessive Force: power, politics & population control*, IPFA Inc. 1995

Infante,D.A. and others, 'Test of an Argumentative Skill Deficiency Model of Interspousal Violence', *Communication Monographs* v56 n2 Jun 1989 p163-177.

Jones,D., *The Black Holocaust: global genocide*, Hikeka Press, 1992

Levinger,G., 'Sources of Marital Dissatisfaction Among Applicants for Divorce', *American Journal of Orthopsychiatry* 36: 803-807 Oct. 1966 in Steinmetz,S.K., p68 in Roy,M., (Ed.)1977 pp63-72

Mama, A., *The Hidden Struggle: statutory and voluntary sector responses to violence against Black women in the home*, London Race and Housing Research Unit, 1989.

Marsden,D., 'Sociological Perspectives on Family Violence', in Martin,J., (ed.), *Violence and the Family*, Wiley,1978.

Mason,A. and Blankenship,V., "Power and Affiliation Motivation, Stress, and Abuse in Intimate Relationships." *Journal of Personality and Social Psychology* 52: 203-210 1987.

McBeth,F., *Violent Treatment*, Public Eye, BBC2 TV 11.12.1992.

Newell,M., (Dir.) and Hampton,C., (writer) *The Good Father*, Film on Four Extra, Channel 4,1986.

Nation of Islam's Historical Research Dept., *The Secret Relationship Between Blacks and Jews*, Vol. 1, Latimer Associates, 1991

Pahl,J., (editor), *Private Violence and Public Policy: The needs of battered women and the response of the public services*, Routledge and Kegan Paul, 1985.

Powers,R.J., "Aggression and Violence in the Family" In, Campbell,A. and Gibbs,J.J., Eds., *Violent Transactions*, Basil Blackwell, 1986.

R,S., *The Human Value*, Sukisa Publications, 1987.

Rodgerson,G. and Wilson,E., (eds.) *Pornography and Feminism: The Case Against Censorship*, Feminists Against Censorship/Lawrence and Wishart, 1991.

Roy,M., (Ed.) *Battered Women: A Psychological Study of Domestic Violence*, Von Nostrand Reinhold, New York 1977.

Steinmetz,S.K., 'Wife Beating, Husband Beating - A comparison of the use of Physical Violence Between Spouses to Resolve Marital Fights', University of Delaware, p68 in Roy,M., (Ed.) *Battered Women: A Psychological Study of Domestic Violence*, Von Nostrand Reinhold, New York 1977 pp63-72 .

Stets,J.E., 'Verbal and Physical Aggression in Marriage', *Journal of Marriage and the Family*, v52 n2 , May 1990

***The** Truth About Sex*, Horizon, BBC 2 TV 3.12.1992.

Williams,C., *The Destruction of Black Civilization: Great Issues of Race from 4500 B.C. to 2000 A.D.*, (2nd edition) Chicago: Third World Press 1988.

Woodcraft,E.(presenter), Dobbs,R.(prod.) and Evans,B.(Dir.), *Do Families Need Fathers?* Maya Vision Productions for Channel 4, 3.12.1992 .

Woodson,C.G., 'The Miseducation of the Negro', *The Crisis*, August 1931 p266

INDEX

MASSIVE 30% DISCOUNT

If you have gained anything from reading **Violation** and you think your friends, family and/or colleagues may also benefit, you can help them and save money at the same time. We offer you a massive 30% discount on any orders of 10 (ten) or more copies of this book. This offer is only available while stocks of this first edition lasts.

....

Please send me .... copies of **VIOLATION**.

I enclose cheque (international money order outside of UK) to the total value of:

A) **£**............ at **£6.59** each in the UK only (this includes over 30% discount plus £1.00 p&p) or

B) US$........... at US$**13.19** each outside the UK (including 30% discount plus $2.00 p&p)

Name ....

Organisation (if any) ....

Address ....

....

....

....

Make cheques payable to:

Sukisa Publications Ltd,

25 Hayter Road,

Brixton, London SW2 5AR.

Tel: 0171 737 8280, Fax: 0171 924 0934

Please allow 14 days for delivery (28 days outside of UK)